Speak

Speak

a short history of languages

TORE JANSON

OXFORD

UNIVERSITY PRESS

OXFORD

UNIVERSITY PRESS

Great Clarendon Street, Oxford OX2 6DP

Oxford University Press is a department of the University of Oxford.
It furthers the University's objective of excellence in research, scholarship,
and education by publishing worldwide in

Oxford New York

Auckland Bangkok Bogotá Buenos Aires Cape Town Chennai
Dar es Salaam Delhi Hong Kong Istanbul Karachi Kolkata
Kuala Lumpur Madrid Melbourne Mexico City Mumbai Nairobi
São Paulo Shanghai Singapore Taipei Tokyo Toronto

with an associated company in Berlin

Oxford is a registered trade mark of Oxford University Press
in the UK and in certain other countries

Published in the United States
by Oxford University Press Inc., New York

© Tore Janson 2002

British Library Cataloguing in Publication Data

Data available

Library of Congress Cataloging in Publication Data

Data applied for

ISBN 0–19–829978–8

Typeset in Aldus Centaur MT
by Hope Services (Abingdon) Ltd
Printed in Great Britain
on acid-free paper by
Biddles Ltd., Guildford & King's Lynn

Contents

List of Maps	vi
List of Tables	vi
Preface	vii
1. Languages Before History	1
2. The Large Language Groups	29
3. Writing and the Egyptians	57
4. Greek and the Greeks	69
5. Latin and the Romans	89
6. Did Dante Write in Italian?	108
7. From Germanic to Modern English	129
8. The Era of National Languages	165
9. Languages of Europe and of the World	184
10. How Languages Are Born—or Made	202
11. How Languages Disappear	232
12. The Heyday of English	251
13. And Then?	267
Suggestions for Further Reading	283
Index	291

LIST OF MAPS

1. The Indo-European languages   37
2. The Bantu languages   45
3. The civilizations of the river valleys   58
4. The Romance languages   117
5. The languages of Britain in Bede's time   132
6. Parts of the world in which the native first language is predominantly European   194

LIST OF TABLES

2.1. A sentence in four languages   29
2.2. Modern and older forms of words in Germanic languages   32
2.3. Similar words in three Slavic languages   33
2.4. Similar words in four Romance languages   34
2.5. Similar words in six old languages   36
2.6. Singular and plural forms in Setswana   48
10.1. The verb "to be" in English, Dutch, and Afrikaans   218
11.1. Geographic distribution of living languages in the year 2000   240

Preface

Two thousand years ago, English did not yet exist. Now it is in use, but some time in the future it will no longer be spoken. The same goes for all languages: they appear, they are used for a time, and they disappear. But there are vast differences between them. Some are just used for a few generations while others exist for millennia. Some languages are spoken by only a handful of people, others are used by hundreds of millions.

How languages arise and vanish, and why languages have such different destinies are issues that have to do with what happens to the people who use the languages. In other words, languages depend on history. But historical events also often depend on which languages people speak. Thus, history is affected by languages, and languages are a part of history.

The role of languages in history is the subject of this book, written for all those who take an interest in languages and in history. Several periods of history and many languages are brought into the discussion, to show how languages and history have interacted and still interact under different circumstances. The book begins in the very distant past and moves on through time all the way to the distant future. A number of examples are introduced, chosen according to what may be interesting and possibly entertaining within the areas I happen to know something about.

These examples are intended to illustrate some of the major trends in the relations between languages and history. This is no trivial task, for there are few generally acknowledged ideas about those relations. The border area between history and linguistics is a rather neglected field of research, and there exist few if any attempts at overview. What is said in this book about the main trends stems largely from the experience of the author.

Learning something about how languages relate to history may be of some use when considering the present and the future. At this very time, the relations between languages are changing profoundly in many parts of the world. The English language is advancing at the expense of a large number of other languages. That development is discussed towards the end of this book. To understand what is really happening and to judge its importance and consequences, it may be useful to see the present in the perspective of what has already happened. That perspective is what I hope this volume will provide.

T.J.

Stockholm
May 2001

ACKNOWLEDGEMENT

Map 1 is taken from *Introduction to the Languages of the World* by Anatole Lyovin, copyright © 1997 by Anatole V. Lyovin. Used by permission of Oxford University Press, Inc.

Map 2 is adapted from *International Encyclopedia of Linguistics (4 Volumes)* by William Bright, copyright © 1992 by Oxford University Press, Inc. Used by permission of Oxford University Press, Inc.

Chapter 1
Languages Before History

WHEN DID LANGUAGES COME INTO BEING?

From Genesis, the first book of the Bible, the reader may infer that Adam was able to speak as soon as he had been created, for he was given a task at once: "And out of the ground the Lord God formed every beast of the field, and every fowl of the air; and brought them unto Adam to see what he would call them; and whatsoever Adam called every living creature, that was the name thereof."

To name the animals, and in that way to invent part of the language, was Adam's first duty. Still, he did not create language as such. It came into being several days before he did, as can be deduced. Almost the first thing that happens in the Bible, at dawn on the first day, is that God says "Let there be light." Evidently, God was able to speak from the very beginning.

Even if we do not accept this version of creation, the text merits consideration for it reveals something of how people tend to think about language and our relation to it.

In the first place, it is remarkable that Adam was created with language built in, as it were. It would have been quite possible to imagine that man was created first and language was added later on. Children cannot speak at birth, and humans in the primordial state could have been speechless like children. Instead, it is precisely the capacity to speak and to name that is represented as specifically human in the narration of the Bible. That capacity makes all the difference in relation to the animals, who have to receive their names from man. Adam is superior to the animals, and language is his instrument of domination.

Secondly, God himself speaks at the very beginning. This may also seem somewhat strange, for he had no one to talk to. On the other hand, it would be even stranger to imagine a dumb God. It is not easy to envision a divinity that resembles man in any way without assuming that this being can speak. It is not necessary, of course, to believe that the god is intelligible. He or she may speak some other, more exalted language than the ones used by humans. But a god who did not speak at all would be a fool or an animal. A being who is human, or superior to man, must master man's most important faculty: language.

Nowadays we believe that our species was not created in a moment but developed from earlier forms that were more similar to apes than we are. But at what point in time did humans actually become human? In other words, when did the earlier forms become so similar to us that we are willing to admit that they were of the same kind as we are?

An answer quite often suggested is to propose that humans became human exactly when language appeared, and this is in fact quite in line with the narration of the Bible. It is natural for us to think that humans are beings who possess a human language.

This does not provide us with a precise answer to the question of when humans first appeared. We do not know when the first utterance was spoken. It is true that many gifted people from antiquity onwards have tried to figure out when and how this happened, but the results are not impressive.

We can be absolutely sure that human languages have existed for at least five thousand years, since this is the approximate age of the first surviving written representations of language. The languages first used in writing, Sumerian and Egyptian, do not differ at all from languages spoken today in their general properties. It seems certain that there have been languages of the kind spoken today for a much longer time.

How long is not at all clear. There are no direct clues, and so all suggestions are speculative. Mainly, people have tried to find a reasonable answer by using two kinds of evidence. One is information about the general cultural development of man in prehistoric times. This is provided by archaeological findings, artefacts of many kinds. The other kind of fact is about the anatomical development of man. Again, archaeology supplies material in the form of bones from different periods.

FORTY THOUSAND OR TWO MILLION YEARS?

Archaeology can tell what tools, made of stone or bones, were used in different periods. Further, there are sculptures, engravings, and paintings that can be dated. From this material it is possible to draw the conclusion that during the last forty thousand years or so, humans seem to have had the same capacity for invention and the same creativity found among (some) modern people. For example, they have been able to invent tools and to create works of art. From this it is generally inferred that at least during this period people have also been using languages with the same basic features as the ones used today. Before that, for a period of around two million years, stone tools were made, and gradually became more sophisticated. However, there are few signs that the people who made them were trying in any way to express themselves artistically.

Thus the archaeological evidence clearly suggests that languages with grammars and vocabularies similar to today's have been spoken for at least 40,000 years. If those who make tools have to be able to speak, languages must have existed for much longer, conceivably as long as a couple of million years. But no one knows whether there really is such a connection between the two skills.

The experts on the anatomy of premodern humans contend that the type of people that exists now, *Homo sapiens sapiens*, has not changed in any substantial way for about 100,000 or 150,000 years. This means, among other things, that during this period people have been equipped with the same type of brain and speech organs as we have today, so presumably neither intellectual nor anatomical problems prevented them from using languages. Their tongues were as mobile as ours, their larynges had vocal cords just like ours, and their brains were equipped with all those amazing convolutions we know are needed in order to speak and to understand speech.

In earlier periods this was not necessarily so. Before the appearance of *Homo sapiens sapiens*, and for some time after that, there were Neanderthal men. Their brains were at least as large as ours are, on average, but the form of their skulls and jaws differed from ours in some respects. This may have prevented them from pronouncing certain speech sounds that are in common use now. However, this is by no means certain, since the remains of Neanderthal people consist only of fragments of bones, and speech is produced through activities in the soft tissue of the mouth and throat. Scholars who work with this problem therefore have to calculate the shape of the soft tissue from the shape of the bones, which is quite difficult. The types of humans who existed before Neanderthal man had bones in the head that differed even further from ours, so it is more probable that they could not speak like us for physiological reasons.

The net result of all this, then, is that we can be reasonably certain that languages like the ones we use have existed for at least 40,000 years, but that they may have been in use for much longer. The upper limit is about 2,000,000 years ago, that is, around the time when man first began to produce stone tools.

WHAT WAS THE REASON?

Thus there is an answer of sorts to the question of when language first appeared. It is of course related to the second question, how languages originated. That problem is even more difficult.

Human languages are the most highly developed and the most flexible systems for communication we know of. The distinctive feature of those systems is that they can be used to convey messages of any degree of complexity in an incredibly swift and efficient manner.

What makes our languages so completely different from the means of communication that are used by other mammals is their degree of complexity, their variability, and their adaptability. Still, there are certain similarities. The signals we employ are sounds produced through the mouth. The air we breathe out is used to create resonance in the upper respiratory tract. Most mammals use the same principle for their production of sounds. Dogs bark, cats meow, mice squeak, horses neigh, and monkeys chatter. All these sounds are made in basically the same manner. Since so many genetically related species produce sounds in a similar way it seems probable that the precursors of man did so too, long before our species had developed.

The sounds of other mammals are also signals, and they are used for contacts with other individuals belonging to the species. They differ from our languages primarily in that their systems for signalling meaning are not very highly developed. It is true that each species can produce several different kinds of sound, and in that way they can to some extent convey different messages. A dog has at its disposal a number of calls to express different attitudes such as threat, fear, sympathy, and so on. People who study communication among animals have found that many species have tens of different signals. Several species of monkey possess fairly large systems, comprising many tens of distinctive sounds. Interestingly, our closest relatives, the chimpanzees, do not seem to use sounds for communication in any way more advanced than many monkeys.

Human speech differs from the cries of other species in many ways. One very important distinction is that all other animals use one call for one message as the general principle of communication. This means that the number of possible messages is very restricted. If a new message is to be included in the system, a new sound has to be introduced, too. After the first few tens of sounds it becomes difficult to invent new distinctive sounds, and also to remember them for the next time they are needed.

Human speech builds on the principle of combining a restricted number of sounds into an unlimited number of messages. In a typical human language there are something like thirty or forty distinctive speech sounds. These sounds can be combined into chains to form a literally unlimited number of words. Even a small child, who can communicate by only one word at a time, uses a system for communication that is infinitely superior to any system utilized by any other animal. The number of words is unlimited, while other species have a very restricted number of signals.

In addition to this, human languages also allow several words to be combined into an utterance. Through this process we are able to create an infinite number of sentences with even a small number of words. This basic property of our languages allows them to express ideas that can be as complex and as subtle as anyone wants. The system has no theoretical limit as to what messages can be conveyed. In principle, everything can be said.

No one knows why or how this marvellous system came about. It is obvious that it must have involved some evolution of the species, as no other animals talk, but all humans do. For more than a century, questions about ultimate causes for evolution have been discussed within the Darwinian framework. That is, the basic assumption is that the capacity for language has evolved because of evolutionary pressure. There had to be some decisive advantage for those individuals who could express themselves well and understand the expressions of others.

Surprisingly, there is still no agreement on what this advantage might have been. Since people speak to each other, it should somehow reasonably be connected with social relations (although even that has been contested). It might be natural to think that with language, people cooperate better within their group, and that gives an advantage to the group. However, that answer is not in line with modern Darwinist thinking, according to which the evolutionary advantage has to favour an individual, and not a group. This is because only an individual, not a group, can transmit a trait to her or his offspring.

For this reason, evolutionary theory runs into difficulties with language, as with much other co-operative behaviour. Recent proposals to solve the dilemma are that language evolved because people who can speak can gain advantages by lying; because people can position themselves in society by providing others with gossip; or because they can develop rituals that work to their advantage. The best I can say about these ideas is that they are difficult to disprove. In the absence of good evidence, speculation will probably continue.

It seems impossible to know, then, why language developed. Thoughts about how it developed are only slightly less speculative. But it may well be that the two fundamental properties of languages developed in sequence. In that case, the first step was the technique of employing a limited number of sounds for an unlimited number of words. This technique may have developed gradually over a very long time.

A language of that kind might have been very useful. As long as one is content to talk about what is important here and now, isolated words might work quite well: "Deer," "Throw!" "Good!" "Cut!" "Fry!" "Sleep," and so on. There are taciturn people nowadays who prefer to speak in that manner, if they have to speak at all, and usually one is quite able to understand what they mean.

Problems arise if one wants to speak about something that is not there to be seen. For example, if one wants to tell a companion to come down the valley to pick raspberries in a new place, it may not be sufficient to say "Raspberries!" It may be necessary to say and point, or to combine two spoken messages: "Raspberries! Go!" or "Raspberries! There!" or something similar. This opens the road towards two-word utterances, and from there on to complete sentences with pronouns, mood, subordination, and other refinements. This cannot have happened all at once, but probably languages developed gradually over many, many thousands of years. At last languages reached such a level that they could be used for unambiguous conversation about the future and the past and about what could be as well as about what really is.

If this was so, our ancestors may have communicated in a more advanced way than any other species for millions of years, even if human languages as we know them have not existed for more than a fraction of that time. Perhaps a very long time was needed for the development of language. That time may have been long enough for changes to be effected in the speech organs and in the brain.

9

This means that the ability to use words may have developed gradually around the time when stone tools came into use, between one and two million years ago. Utterances consisting of several words may have appeared much later. The full development of speech systems, with embedded clauses and other complexities, may have been completed less than a hundred thousand years ago.

However this may have been, it seems certain that the kind of languages we use existed for at least 40,000 years. This means that in the Early Iron Age, when all human beings lived as gatherers and hunters and used tools made of bone and stone, languages were fully developed and could have had large vocabularies, complex sentences, and all other features that are found in languages of today.

THE LANGUAGES OF GATHERERS AND HUNTERS

In and around the Kalahari Desert in southern Africa live people traditionally called Bushmen in English. In recent years, the term used to designate this group is San. Up to a generation ago, many San people lived on what they could get through hunting and through gathering edible roots and fruits. They owned nothing beyond the loincloth that they wore and the few weapons and utensils that they carried. Some very small groups still live more or less in this way, as did all human beings up to about ten thousand years ago, when agriculture first appeared.

The San people and their culture, as well as similar groups in other parts of the world, tell us something about what life may have been like for most of the time during which man has existed. Of course, not all hunters and gatherers lived in the same way, for there were certainly great variations over the world due to climate, availability of food, and local traditions. Still one may draw some conclusions about the life of gatherers and hunters in earlier ages from studying San and other present-day gatherers and hunters.

Right now, the life of the San people is changing very rapidly. Owing to contacts with modern society, their traditional lifestyle is disappearing. Their new situation is very problematic, and may bring about the disappearance of their very cultural identity, and also their languages. Here I will discuss only the traditional life and languages of the San peoples, disregarding the great changes of recent decades.

The languages of the San peoples form a group that is usually called Khoisan. One of the languages of this group, Nama (or Khoekhoegowab) is spoken by more than a hundred thousand sedentary people in Namibia, but they are not included in the following comments. There are several other Khoisan languages. The total number of people speaking these languages is about seventy thousand, which means that fairly few people speak each language.

These languages have not been well described. On the whole they are not used in writing and exist only as spoken languages. The speakers have lived in relative isolation in or near the desert. But some missionaries, anthropologists, and linguists have studied and described several of these languages. This is no easy task, as I quickly learned in some feeble attempts of my own. The first problem is to establish contacts between people with fundamentally different languages and different cultures, who may also have different attitudes towards the contact itself. A linguist should preferably live with the speakers for a year or longer in order to make a full and reliable description. But that is usually impossible for practical reasons. Among those who are still gatherers and hunters, the very presence of a researcher is both a problem and a big change. The ones who live as farm labourers close to the desert are generally beset by serious problems. They need teachers, health care, and social workers much more than they need people who ask about their way of talking.

In spite of such problems we now know a great deal about the Khoisan languages. We can build on that knowledge to make some informed guesses about the linguistic situation during most of the time human beings of our kind have existed.

WERE LANGUAGES THEN JUST LIKE LANGUAGES NOW?

The first and most important thing that has to be said about languages in societies of gatherers and hunters is that there is in principle no difference between these and other languages. It is often believed that languages spoken in societies where the material culture is not highly developed are also simpler and in some way less developed than the language we speak. Many linguists thought so in the nineteenth century. But this is not true.

This requires some explanation, and certain reservations should be made. What does it mean to say that a language is developed, or that it is not developed? One may think of various properties of languages when making this kind of judgement. One may think about the linguistic system, that is to say the sounds, the word forms, and the way sentences are formed. Further one may think of the vocabulary, if there are words and expressions to denote everything that needs to be said and understood, if it is possible to express subtle shades of meaning and if the same thing can be said in several different ways. And finally one may think of the written language and its tradition, how many books are published in the language, if there are good authors who have written in the language, and so on.

When linguists maintain that Khoisan languages, or American Indian languages, are just as developed as the large European languages, what they are talking about is the linguistic system. All the fundamental features of spoken languages all over the world are the same. Each language has a set of distinctive sounds that are combined into meaningful words. Each language has ways to denote grammatical notions like person ("I, you, he"), singular or plural, present or past time, and more. Each language also has rules governing how the words are to be combined to form complete utterances.

In their details languages differ greatly, as is well known. It is not true that all languages are equally difficult at all levels, a fact easy to observe by any language learner. For example, the English language has a highly elaborated system of vowels and diphthongs, while Spanish has only five basic vowels. On the other hand, the verbs in Spanish have many more forms than the verbs in English. Any attempt to make a comprehensive assessment of the difficulty or the "development" of these two languages would entail a decision about whether vowels contribute more to difficulty than verb forms, or vice versa. It is very hard to find criteria for such decisions. In their totality, both languages are highly complex and very difficult to master. This does not necessarily mean that all languages are at exactly the same level when it comes to difficulty or development in this sense, but it is hard to find major differences.

The Khoisan languages all have very complex sound systems. They have more vowels and many more consonants than is found in any European language. This is partly because all these languages have special consonants, called clicks; they are used as speech sounds only in southern Africa. In addition, they use more consonants than we do even if the clicks are not counted. One Khoisan language, called !Xóõ, has a larger number of speech sounds than any other known language. There are more than a hundred distinctive sounds, as compared with thirty or forty in most other languages. On the other hand, both in !Xóõ and in many other Khoisan languages the number of different forms for each verb is small, and the rules for sentence formation are mostly simple. So those language systems are difficult as far as the sounds are concerned, but fairly simple in other ways.

This is not true for languages used among gatherers and hunters in other parts of the world. The Australian Aborigines spoke many different languages when the Europeans arrived. Most of these are very simple as far as the sound systems are concerned. Several of them have less than twenty distinctive sounds, which is about as low as is reported for any human language. But their systems for inflecting words are very advanced, so that one single complex verb may sometimes express a meaning that has to be rendered by several clauses in English. An example from the Australian language Rembarrnga is *yarran-*

məʔ-kuʔpi-popna-ni-yuwa. This form with six components is to be understood, according to the leading authority, R. M. W. Dixon, as "it [the kangaroo] might smell our sweat as we try to sneak up on it." So the Australian languages are simple when it comes to sounds, but difficult at other levels.

This shows that languages in cultures of gatherers and hunters are just like other languages in terms of sounds and grammar: they are simple in some ways, and complex in others, just like English or Spanish or Arabic. As far as the language systems are concerned, the languages we speak are fully comparable with the languages spoken among gatherers and hunters of today, and presumably with those spoken by our ancestors when they were gatherers and hunters. On average, languages do not become more or less complex. They just vary.

VOCABULARY AND SOCIETY

When it comes to vocabulary, and the possibilities to express concepts, the situation is different. The capacity to create new words or to borrow words from other languages exists in all languages of the world, so in theory each language can have words for everything. But in practice the vocabularies of languages often differ greatly. The words and expressions in use in a language are those needed and adequate in the culture within which the language is spoken. Languages used in very diverse cultures therefore have very diverse vocabularies.

The vocabulary of a Khoisan language, for example Juǀ'hoan, is just the vocabulary needed by hunters and gatherers in and around the Kalahari Desert. There are many names for animals and plants, including some that may not have names of their own in any other language. Words for human relations and for human emotions are at least as numerous as in European languages, and so are, of course, words for the parts of the human body, for life and death, and so on. There are also many words that can be used in mythical narratives and for religious concepts. Generally speaking the language possesses rich resources for expression of all that is normally spoken about in the environment where it is used.

But much that is found in European languages has been lacking in Ju|'hoan until the last few decades. Of course there have been no words to denote modern technology, such as cars or television, but there have also been no words for many things we regard as familiar and obvious, such as houses, furniture, household utensils, and clothes. As the San people have lived in small groups without permanent leaders there are no traditional words that have to do with state or constitution, law or police. They have not conducted any wars, so there have been no words for generals, troops, or cannons.

In the society of San people there has been little need for mathematics, since they have had neither cattle nor money, nor anything else that has to be counted. This is reflected in the language, which lacks inherited words for plus or minus, and is by no means rich in numerals. There seem to be no special words in Ju|'hoan for numbers higher than 6.

There is another reason why one finds fewer words and expressions in Khoisan languages than in English and in other European languages: there is no written language. For this reason the language, including all the words, can be transferred from one generation to the next only through the children's learning to understand and speak it.

This may be of great importance, especially for a language that is used by relatively few people. A word denoting something that is not frequently spoken about may not be learnt by all people, but only by some. If there are no more than a few thousand, or even a few hundred speakers, the risk that an uncommon word will not be transmitted at all can be considerable, and in that case it is irretrievably lost. When someone needs to talk about this again it will be necessary to use a circumlocution of some kind, or to invent a new word. How much this type of vocabulary loss happens in practice cannot be known, as it is hardly possible to study the process directly. But there is considerable evidence that people who use written language get support from it, so that their vocabulary is richer also when they talk.

A language without a written form also runs a considerable risk of losing poems and other linguistic artefacts. It is not that literature cannot exist without writing. There are abundant examples of poems transmitted orally, including very long epic tales. But this requires that at least a few people in each generation can devote themselves to the task of memorizing and performing the material. In a small group of speakers, this may not happen, and in that case, words and expressions are not transmitted to later generations by way of extensive literary works.

In summary, languages of gatherers and hunters are just like European languages in terms of their fundamental properties and capacity for expression, but this capacity is not used in the same way. As their languages are not used in the same situations as ours are, their resources for expression are also different. They possess all the words and expressions that are needed by the societies in which they are used, including much that is not found in European languages, but much is lacking that seems quite basic to us.

Clearly, this has nothing to do with the structure or the potential of the languages, but only with what they are used for. At present the Ju|'hoan speakers are creating or borrowing many words denoting things and concepts of the modern world. In that way they adapt their language to a new situation. This is perfectly possible, and there is no theoretical reason why Ju|'hoan could not in the future be used for discussions about polymer chemistry or computer design. In the same way, speakers of English could adapt their language to allow for discussions about plants and hunting in the Kalahari. However, the process of building a vocabulary is slow and laborious. Therefore, users of Ju|'hoan will be at a disadvantage in many urban contexts for a long time. English will hardly ever be adapted to the situation in the desert.

HOW MANY KHOISAN LANGUAGES ARE THERE?

The Khoisan languages, spoken by the San peoples, are fairly numerous. It is by no means an easy matter to find out how many they are or what they are called. A person who starts studying what has been written about these languages is liable to get confused very soon. Everyone who tries to describe the situation offers a large number of language names, most of them spelt in remarkable ways.

These strange spellings are partly but not completely explained by the difficulty of rendering the click sounds in writing. Clicks are sounds formed by creating low pressure in the mouth and then letting the air in abruptly. Such sounds are often used for special purposes in other parts of the world. By speakers of English, for example, it is not unusual to signal disapproval or disbelief through a sound that is often transcribed "tut" or "tut-tut." This is in fact the sound called a dental click in Khoisan languages. But there, it is used within words as an ordinary consonant, and there are also other clicks that sound different. To denote these sounds in writing, different systems can be used. Usually, linguists employ the symbols | and ! and ‡ and ⊙.

One of the important scholars within the field of Khoisan languages, Dorothea Bleek from Germany, reported in the 1950s that there are about twenty different languages, with names such as |*Xam*, ‡*Khomani*, ||*K'au*||*en*, and !*Kuŋ*. Almost no other author uses exactly those names. Instead of the last one, one may find for example !*Xu*, !*Khung*, *Kung*, and !*Kung*.

This would only be a minor problem if it were just a matter of differences in spelling. But for several decades almost all scholars who have been working with Khoisan languages have also added one or several names of languages or dialects. In 1981, an energetic scholar published a list of most of the names of Khoisan languages that had been used up to that time in the scholarly literature. The list includes a total of 141 items, disregarding minor variations in spelling. Since that time, a few more have been proposed.

There is probably no one who believes that there are as many different languages as that among 70,000 speakers or thereabouts. The typical situation is that there are many names for what most people agree is actually one language. Just as an example, for a language which is often called *Shuakhwe*, the following names have also been used, among others: ǁ’*Ayè*, *Danisa*, ǁ*Koreekhoe*, |*Xaise*, *Tçaiti*, *Hura*, *Teti*, !*Hukwe*.

There are several reasons why the list of names has become so long. Several names refer to languages and groups that no longer exist. Many people who spoke Khoisan languages lived in the southern and eastern parts of South Africa. They were persecuted in atrocious ways, and in some cases actual genocide was committed. The remnants of those peoples gave up their languages and started using a form of Afrikaans. The Khoisan languages in South Africa are now extinct. About forty of the names refer to them.

Still, there are just too many remaining names. To understand why this is so we have to discuss the languages themselves and their relation to each other.

"WHAT LANGUAGE DO YOU SPEAK?" "DON'T KNOW."

Linguistic studies of Khoisan languages have shown that the group consists of three very dissimilar subgroups. As a matter of fact, they are so different that it is not even certain that they are related. The three families are Northern Khoisan, Central Khoisan, and Southern Khoisan. The Southern Khoisan group nowadays comprises only one language. It would therefore seem quite easy to tell the name of that language, but it is not.

Here, we meet the real problem concerning language names. It turns out that the speakers themselves, when asked about the name of their language, do not produce an unambiguous answer. This is not because they are slow on the uptake or because of communication problems. The reason is simply that no answer is to be had. This language just does not have a name in the language. That this is so has been established without doubt by Anthony Traill, one of the few scholars who has learnt a Khoisan language thoroughly and is able to speak it.

We may be somewhat slow in absorbing this fact. At any rate, the scholars, missionaries, and others who have been in touch with these languages have not understood it for a long time. This may be the most important reason why one finds such an excessive number of names in the literature. Each eager explorer has asked the people what language they speak. The persons asked have tried to formulate a suitable answer, which has been conscientiously written down by the scholar. The next scholar has met some other speaker, who has produced some other polite answer, and that too has been recorded for posterity. In that way the number of reported Khoisan languages has constantly grown larger, from the mid-nineteenth century until a decade or two ago.

Several questions may be asked about this. The first one is what kind of names scholars have actually recorded. It turns out that most of them belong to one of three types. First, there are words that denote a larger group to which the speaker belongs. Those are the most stable names, which tend to recur in many variants, and they mean at least partly the same as our language names. But even if a person regards herself or himself as belonging to a group that has a name, this does not necessarily mean that all people who talk the same language belong to that group. There may be others who talk in the same way but do not belong to the group. Also, it is quite possible for people who talk in slightly different ways, or even in very different ways, to regard themselves as belonging to one group with one name.

The second type of name denotes the area where the speakers live, or the family or small group to which the speaker belongs. That is as if English was called the Luton language or the Smith language. Such designations tend to lengthen the list of existing names in a very confusing way.

The third type of name is represented by such as *Kwe*, *Khoe*, *Shuakhwe*, *‖Anikhwe*, and also by the term *Khoisan*, which has been fabricated by Europeans from words taken from the languages. All these words consist of or contain the same word stem *khwe* or *khwi*, which consists of two sounds, an aspirated *k*-sound which is pronounced with rounded lips, and a front vowel, *e* or *i*. The word means "human being" or "people." The people who have been asked have answered that they speak the language of humans, or that they speak as people do.

The next question is how it is possible that people have not got a name for the language they speak. To us, it seems self-evident that a person must know which language she or he is speaking. But if one thinks of the environment in which those languages have been used, the explanation is quite obvious. The San people have lived in small groups of ten or twenty people, and each group has been out of contact with other groups during most of the year. During some periods they have met other people, both for trade and for other common activities. But there has not been any state, or union, or other common institution causing the people who talk in a similar way to regard themselves as a separate unit or group. The groups that people have felt they belong to have mostly been much smaller than any imagined group of all people speaking the same language. In such a situation, the language has no particular importance for a person's identity or status, and therefore does not have to have a name of its own.

Finally, one may ask what should be done by outside observers when the speakers themselves do not provide us with a name for their language. The answer is of course that nothing prevents us from introducing one. That is precisely what linguists have done. When it comes to the Southern Khoisan language I have discussed, most linguists agree now that it should be called !Xóõ.

So far, the matter is not very difficult, since this southern language is fairly homogeneous, without any major dialectal differences, and it is clearly different from all other languages. The northern group, on the other hand, consists of one or two or three languages, depending on whether one regards differences between speakers as dialectal differences or differences in language. As for the Central Khoisan languages, the situation is even less clear. It is a certain fact that there are a number of languages that are not at all mutually intelligible. On the other hand, all the languages are related, and some are quite similar. In several cases it is not obvious whether it is better to talk about different dialects or about different languages.

WHAT IS A LANGUAGE?

At this point we again encounter the question of what a language is. It reappears time and again in this book. As a preliminary, it should be said that there are few generally accepted rules or criteria for deciding when two ways of speaking should be regarded as being the same language and when they should be seen as two separate ones.

Obviously, when two forms of speech are so dissimilar that it is completely impossible to establish communication, as is the case with English and Chinese, for example, they are regarded as different languages by everyone. Further, people who understand each other are usually regarded as speaking the same language, and those who speak the same language are supposed to understand each other. But here, there are many exceptions. For example, Swedes and Norwegians usually understand each other without difficulty, but Swedish and Norwegian are regarded as different languages. On the other hand, many Americans from the Midwest do not understand Londoners, and vice versa, but they are supposed to be using the same English language. This is why it is necessary to rely on the speakers themselves in dubious cases.

When it comes to the Khoisan languages, it is not possible to ask. The speakers in some cases have no names at all for their languages, nor of course for dialects. So, this whole line of reasoning is without meaning for them until the Westernized way of thinking about languages has been taken over into their culture. This has not happened yet, at least not generally. For this reason there is simply no answer to the question of how many Khoisan languages there are. Within certain limits, there are as many languages as scholars and state authorities decide.

HOW MANY LANGUAGES EXISTED
TWELVE THOUSAND YEARS AGO?

Even if we cannot tell precisely whether there are ten or fifteen or perhaps twenty Khoisan languages, it is still clear that there are many quite different languages. It is remarkable for people who are accustomed to the situation in Europe, not to mention America, that a group as small as 70,000 people uses so many different languages. In Europe, the large languages are spoken by tens of millions of people and the whole of Western Europe with several hundred million speakers only has about fifty languages (not counting languages spoken by immigrants who have arrived during the last generation).

It should be noted in passing that the phrase "large languages" in the previous sentence is just a shorter way of saying "languages used by many persons." Similarly, "small languages" are languages used by few. For the sake of convenience those phrases and their counterparts in the singular are used freely in this book. Of course they do not imply any judgement of value.

The fact that there is such a difference in the number of speakers is of course no coincidence. It is directly related to the great differences between Europeans and San people in culture and lifestyle, and also in the way they use languages.

The San people, who live (or have lived) on what they can get from hunting and gathering fruits and edible roots, need large areas to provide themselves with food. Even in a relatively fertile area, a square kilometre of land can support only a few people. In the Kalahari Desert, where the San people live, even more space is needed. This means that each group needs a large area, and has to move over it systematically. They cannot live close to other people. There are not many reasons to get in touch with people other than those belonging to neighbouring groups. Thus, each group is comparatively isolated.

Each group of course uses a language. It is a well-known fact that languages are never transmitted in exactly the same shape from generation to generation; they change over time. If a group of people has few contacts with others speaking its language, a separate speech form will soon appear. This is what we call a dialect. If this process is allowed to run its course for a few centuries, the group may develop a language that is incomprehensible to all other people.

This should mean that in times and places where people constantly live in small groups without contacts, far from each other, there will appear many languages with few speakers. This seems to be true for the situation among San people. The next question is whether this was also so at the time when all people on earth were gatherers and hunters.

Actually, the known facts indicate strongly that this was the case. For in other parts of the world where there have recently been sizeable populations of gatherers and hunters, the situation is quite similar. The aborigines of Australia are thought to have spoken about 270 languages when the Europeans arrived. They are now only about fifty thousand people. It is true that they were much more numerous two hundred years ago, when the Europeans started occupying their land, but even if they were ten times as many, there were still no more than a couple of thousand speakers for each language, on average. Among Indians in the

Amazon region, the situation is similar. There are no indications anywhere that gatherers and hunters usually have languages that are spoken by more than a few thousand people.

If this is correct, it means that we can say something about how many languages existed in the world at the time when all people were hunters and gatherers, 12,000 years ago or thereabouts. According to the discussion above, one has to conclude that at that time there was about one language for every thousand or two thousand people.

The next question, of course, is how many people there were. We do not know that. On the other hand we know that there were human beings on all continents in most of the areas that are densely populated now. There cannot possibly have been just a few thousand people altogether; the number has to be in the millions. Just to take an example, if there were ten million people, and 2,000 persons to each language, there would have been 5,000 languages.

There is probably no way to find out what the correct population figure is, although archaeologists and demographers have made certain calculations. But it is interesting to compare the example with the number of languages found nowadays. According to most estimates, the figure is around 6,000, or at least of that order of magnitude.

This means that there may actually have been as many languages on earth at the time of gatherers and hunters as are found today, even though the population at that period was not much larger than 10,000,000, that is only about two-tenths of 1 per cent of the present population of more than five billion people.

These figures should not be taken very seriously, as they are based on a number of premises, which are far from certain. But there is hardly any doubt about the general trend. In early times there were lots of languages, very many more than now in relative terms, and perhaps more than now even in absolute numbers. The history of languages by no means entails that the number of languages increases. On the contrary, the general trend is certainly that the number of languages has fallen, at least relatively speaking. This is quite important to our understanding of the role of languages and of linguistic differences. Several chapters in this book take that observation as their starting-point.

The next chapter, however, is about language groups. Why is it that some languages are similar, and others are not?

Chapter 2
The Large Language Groups

The English word *bread* corresponds to the German word *Brot*, the Swedish *bröd*, and the Italian word *pane*. The word *son* means the same as German *Sohn*, Swedish *son*, and Italian *figlio*. In both cases, the English, German, and Swedish words are fairly similar, but the Italian ones are completely different.

This is not accidental. English, German, and Swedish are alike in many ways, while Italian is distinct from all of them. This is even more evident if one compares short sentences from each language.

TABLE 2.1. *A sentence in four languages*

English	We could not come
German	Wir konnten nicht kommen
Swedish	Vi kunde inte komma
Italian	Non potevamo venire

In English, German, and Swedish, each single word in the sentence matches one word in the other languages, and the words are in the same order. *We* means the same as *wir* and *vi*, *could* has the same meaning as *konnten* and *kunde*, and so on. But in Italian, the word meaning "not" is first in the sentence, and there is no word that directly corresponds to "we." Instead, the word *potevamo* means "we could," while "they could," for example, would be rendered by *potevano*.

So some languages have much in common, but others differ in very many ways. The reasons for this were discussed briefly in the previous chapter. Languages keep changing all the time. Groups of people who spoke the same language to begin with may become isolated from each other, and after some time they will end up speaking quite different languages due to the independent changes. But languages are also influenced by each other. If two groups of people speaking different languages have been in contact for a long time, their languages will resemble each other in some respects. To begin with, only single words are taken over, but in due time there will be other changes. How extensive these changes become, and which language will be most affected, has to do with the kind of contacts between the groups, and with their respective shares of power and influence. In that way, language changes are connected with history.

The pace of language change is usually rather slow compared to the lifespan of an individual. Old people notice and often complain about some changes from when they were young, but mostly fairly minor issues. A substantial number of foreign words may be introduced to a language in a short time, but the sounds of a language do not normally change fast, and changes in grammar in most cases take even longer. There is no constant rate of change, but often languages remain fairly similar even when they have been separated for more than a millennium, and remain quite different even after an equally long period of contact.

The case of English, German, and Swedish is a typical example of slow divergence. Historians and historical linguists agree that the three languages (and some others, for example Dutch and Danish) have a common origin in one language. This group of languages is called Germanic, and the original language is usually called Proto-Germanic.

No one knows for certain what Proto-Germanic sounded like. It was never written down, and we do not know much about the people who may have spoken this language or precisely when and where it was used. But we do know a good deal about what has happened to the several Germanic languages. The oldest substantial texts in Old English were written about 1,300 years ago, and the first Old German texts are about as old. Thus, it is possible to follow the development of these two languages for many centuries. As for Swedish, it is very closely related to the other Nordic languages Icelandic, Danish, and Norwegian, and the oldest written records, which are short inscriptions from the fourth and fifth centuries AD, are best seen as representing a Proto-Nordic language. The oldest long texts in any Nordic language were written in Iceland in the twelfth century. The language of those texts is called Old Norse.

When comparing Old English, Old German, and Old Norse, one can easily see that those languages were considerably more similar to each other than are their modern counterparts. Table 2.2 gives a few words that can serve as examples.

TABLE 2.2. *Modern and older forms of words in Germanic languages*

English	birds	way	go
German	Vögel	Weg	gehen
Swedish	fåglar	väg	gå
Old English	fugelas	weg	gan
Old High German	fugala	uueg	gangan
Old Norse	fuglar	vegr	ganga

It is clear that the words were closer in form in the old languages. As a matter of fact, the spoken languages were so similar that people from England and from Scandinavia may have been able to understand each other's speech to some extent.

Twelve hundred years ago, then, the languages of much of western and northern Europe were much more alike than they are now. Most historical linguists and historians think that if it were possible to get solid evidence about the language situation around a thousand years before, it would show that the same language, Proto-Germanic, was spoken all over the area.

This is probably correct. But a question follows straight away: why was one language used over such a vast region? This chapter is meant to provide an answer of sorts to this question, and some similar ones. As a matter of fact, there seems to be no very good answer that applies specifically to the Germans. Instead, we will move on to other groups, trying to find a general pattern.

Most European languages belong to one of three major groups. East and south-east of the Germanic languages, there are the Slavic languages. The largest one is Russian, but

Ukrainian, Polish, Belarus, Czech, Serbo-Croatian, Bulgarian, and quite a few smaller languages also belong to the group. Those languages are by and large more alike than are the Germanic ones. Written texts may convey another impression, as some languages, for instance Russian, are written in the Cyrillic alphabet, but others, such as Polish and Czech, in our ordinary Latin script. However, if Russian is transcribed it becomes evident that many words are almost identical, for example the ones for *bread* and *sun* (Table 2.3).

TABLE 2.3. *Similar words in three Slavic languages*

	bread	sun
Russian	xleb	solnche
Polish	chleb	słonce
Czech	chléb	slunce

The first sound in the Russian word for "bread" is a velar fricative, as *ch* in the Scottish word *loch*. It is quite similar to the corresponding sounds in the Polish and Czech words.

There are ancient texts in Slavic languages too, most notably religious texts written in what is usually called Old Church Slavonic and dating from the ninth century and onwards. It is believed that all Slavic languages stem from one Proto-Slavic language, just as the Germanic ones are supposed to derive from Proto-Germanic. Proto-Slavic may have been spoken over a vast area around AD 1.

The third large group of languages in Europe consists of the Romance languages, mainly in southern and western Europe. The most important ones are French, Spanish, Italian, and Portuguese. The words for *bread* and *son* in those languages are shown in Table 2.4.

TABLE 2.4. *Similar words in four Romance languages*

	bread	son
French	pain	fils
Spanish	pan	hijo
Italian	pane	figlio
Portuguese	pão	filho

The words in the four languages are so similar that it is obvious that they cannot have originated independently from one another. As a matter of fact, there is little need to guess about history in the case of those languages. There are many texts from older stages, and we know about their origin. All of them have developed from Latin, which was spoken and written around two thousand years ago in the part of Europe where the Romance languages are found today.

In this case, it is known why one language was used in such a vast territory. To begin with, around 700 or 600 BC, Latin was spoken only in Rome and its immediate environs. But the Romans gradually expanded their realm, and around AD 100 they ruled over all western Europe and the entire

Mediterranean region. After a few centuries their empire vanished, but their language had become the native tongue of the inhabitants in most of the western part.

Did the Germans and the Slavs also rule over large empires? The answer is no. There are no indications that such states ever existed, either in historical sources or in archaeological remains. The Roman rule was unique also in its linguistic significance. The Slavic and Germanic languages must have been spread in some other way. It is necessary to draw even more languages into the picture in order to reach a tentative conclusion as to how that came about.

INDO-EUROPEAN LANGUAGES

The three language groups referred to in the previous section are not unrelated to each other. They resemble each other in several ways, although the similarities are not so obvious as they are within each group.

As we have already seen in the case of Germanic languages, old forms of languages may be more similar to each other than the present-day forms. At Table 2.5 is a list of the words for father and mother from a few old languages of Europe and one old language of India, Sanskrit.

An English scholar in the eighteenth century who devoted himself to Sanskrit studies, Sir William Jones, noted many such similarities and even more striking parallels in grammar. In a famous lecture in Calcutta in 1786 he proposed that Latin, Greek, Sanskrit, the Germanic languages, and the Celtic languages, to which Irish belongs, had a common origin.

TABLE 2.5. *Similar words in six old languages*

	father	mother
Latin	pater	mater
Ancient Greek	pater	meter
Old English	fæder	modor
Old Norse	faðir	moðir
Old Irish	athir	mathir
Sanskrit	pitar	matar

This more or less marked the beginning of historical linguistics. In the following century a large number of scholars proved beyond reasonable doubt that Jones was right, and expanded his original idea to a detailed theory of the relations between many dozens of languages in twelve or thirteen subgroups. The whole group is now generally referred to as the Indo-European languages.

In short, the Indo-European language group consists of the Germanic and Slavic languages, the Italic languages (including Latin, Romance, and a few extinct languages), quite a few other European languages such as Greek, Baltic languages, Celtic languages, Albanian, a number of Iranian languages including Persian (Farsi), and several important languages of India, such as Sanskrit and Hindi. Several Indo-European languages are preserved only in ancient texts, and some have already been mentioned; one may add, among others, Hittite, which was used in present-day Turkey.

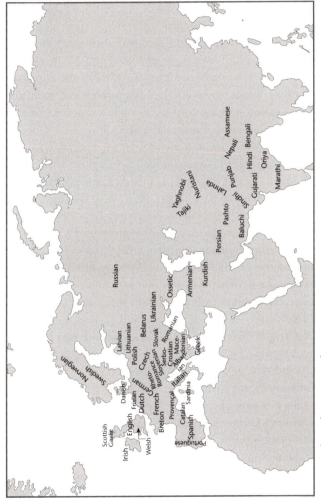

MAP 1. The Indo-European languages

The proofs that all these languages are related have been found by comparing the languages preserved in the oldest texts, such as Sanskrit, Greek, and Latin, with each other and with reconstructed proto-languages such as Proto-Germanic and Proto-Slavic. The results are clear. First, there are important similarities. Secondly, the differences in sounds and grammars are often quite systematic and can be explained as the effects of a fairly small number of general changes.

To illustrate this, one may use an example from Table 2.5. The words for "father" are so similar that they ought to have a common origin. But one difference is that the Germanic languages, that is Old English and Old Norse, have an *f* at the beginning of the word for "father", while the other languages have a *p*. This may seem to weaken the idea of a common origin. But if the matter is investigated further, it turns out that this correspondence is found not only in this word, but also in principle for all words that the languages have in common. Another example is English *fish*, which corresponds to Latin *piscis*. The conclusion is that original Indo-European *p-* has changed into *f-* in the Germanic languages. This is a common type of change that has been observed in many other languages. So, what first seemed to be an irregular deviation was found to be an instance of a regular change.

Because of many changes over a long time, there are very great differences between many of the languages. A speaker of English uses an Indo-European language, but will hardly be able to recognize a single word in Persian or Hindi, although those too are Indo-European. The reason is that the languages have been separated for a very long time and have developed along quite disparate paths. Still it is certain that they do belong together.

So the Indo-European languages are really related to each other. They are believed to originate from a common proto-language, usually called Proto-Indo-European.

Let us now get back to the problem brought up earlier: how did these languages propagate? The question becomes even trickier when all Indo-European languages are considered. What is behind the facts that the Germanic and Slavic languages are found over such large areas and that the Indo-European language has off-shoots that are spoken all over Europe and large parts of Asia?

Several answers have been proposed. In any case, the way of life must have been an important factor. As early as several thousand years ago it had changed much from the culture of gatherers and hunters.

From around 10,000 years ago people began to influence vegetation by sowing and reaping sought-after plants. In addition, people started to domesticate animals and send them out to pasture. It seems as if those changes were brought about independently in several places on earth: in the Near East, in China, and in present Mexico. In each centre, different plants and animals were involved. If this really happened without mutual contacts it is a very remarkable matter. On the other hand it is also very hard to figure out how any contacts could have been established, in particular between Central America and Asia. This is one of the many mysteries of the distant past. In addition, there were other centres, such as West Africa, Ethiopia, New Guinea, and the Andes, which may have got the general idea from elsewhere but used indigenous plants and animals.

In a complex series of events, farming and herding spread from all these centres to other parts of the world at a very uneven pace. Archaeologists date the earliest certain traces of farming to around 10,000 years ago in the Near East, and just slightly later in China.

As the new techniques were introduced, people's mode of existence was altered drastically, for several reasons.

In the first place, agriculture and stock-raising can provide food for many more people. A rough rule of thumb says that gatherers and hunters need ten times as much land as farmers do, even if the methods of agriculture are primitive. So, when agriculture is introduced the population can grow greatly.

This was no sudden process. The new modes of food production have been spreading slowly over the world for several thousand years, and have actually just barely reached some areas. Therefore, the population expanded at widely differing times in different parts of the world. In the Mediterranean and in Europe, and also in India and China, the expansion happened several thousand years ago. In these regions, the population has been fairly dense for thousands of years. But in Australia and in western North America agriculture was introduced only when the Europeans arrived a few hundred years ago. At that time, the population was very small compared to what it has become since then. In a few places, mainly in Africa and in South America, some people have lived entirely as gatherers and hunters even in the latter half of the twentieth century, and a few may still be left.

Secondly, farming meant that people became much more sedentary. Instead of living in small, mobile groups they settled more permanently where the soil and the climate were suitable. Often many gathered in a small area.

Thirdly, farming and stock-keeping made people owners of land and of animals. That led to disputes, and it became necessary to maintain order. Some kind of law appeared, and enforcement of law. Society became more complex.

Fourthly, relations between groups became more problematic. In societies where something can be owned, surplus is also sometimes created. Those who wield power can get hold of the surplus. One way to wield power is to use force, or to threaten with force. Whether force and war have always been in use is not easy to know, but there is hardly any doubt that when people became owners these activities became much more profitable, and therefore more common. By and by, a technology was also developed. The sword was invented, a weapon that is used against other human beings rather than against beasts. When the horse was domesticated, perhaps 5,000 years ago, it soon became used to pull wagons with armed warriors, a very effective device against people on foot. In this way, wars originated.

So farming and livestock-keeping changed the human condition radically. Life became more sedentary, with many other people in the neighbourhood. Societies became larger, more organized, and more violent.

What in all this was crucial for the spread of some languages and language groups at the expense of others? The question has been asked mainly with regard to the Indo-European languages, but in fact it is relevant for other areas and other language groups too.

For now, we focus on those parts of the world that were affected by the development of agriculture and stock-raising in the Near East. Agriculture first appeared in a region sometimes called the Fertile Crescent, comprising parts of present-day Iraq, Turkey, Syria, and Israel. There are mainly two, rather different attempts to explain how the changes in lifestyle caused the spread of Indo-European languages.

The first one focuses on wars and conquests. Several archaeologists have seen the Indo-Europeans as warriors who expanded their dominion from a small core area somewhere north of the Black Sea to all Europe and half of Asia. This would have happened within a fairly short period of time, beginning around 5,000 years ago. The people who came under their sway abandoned their original tongues and took up the language of the conquerors.

This is certainly a possible sequence of events, and similar things are recorded in history. The rule of Rome was expanded in this way in the course of a few hundred years. Also, the Muslims subdued northern Africa and south-western Asia in the seventh and eighth centuries AD, and after some centuries Arabic became the native language of the people in much of the area.

But actually, the parallel with what might have happened 5,000 years ago is less close than it may appear. The Romans and the Arabs had schools, written languages, and strong states using an official language. All this is known to favour language shift. Conquerors without such assets, such as the Huns under Attila in the fifth century AD, or the Mongols under Genghis Khan in the thirteenth century, have failed to propagate their languages. We can be sure that the Indo-Europeans had no schools, no state bureaucracy, and no written language. So how could their language become so successful over such a vast area with so many people in a relatively short time-span? There is no easy answer to that question, and it is tempting to speculate about alternative explanations.

This brings us to the second main approach. It was suggested by the British archaeologist Colin Renfrew in the 1980s, and has caused a great deal of debate. According to Renfrew, the decisive factor was not conquest, but the spread of farming. Archaeological findings show that the new technology expanded slowly from the Near East over south-east Europe and reached southwestern and northern Europe only after several thousand years. As has been pointed out, this technological advance also brought about a large increase of the population. Renfrew's idea is quite simply that the people who introduced farming spoke the Indo-European language. It soon developed into different Indo-European languages because of the incessant process of change that has been mentioned.

If this was so, there is no need to assume any great wars or conquests. The newcomers just ousted the few gatherers and hunters because of their large numbers and their new mode of production. And the land was not usually taken in war. Rather, the many children of the farmers took possession of uncultivated land close to that of their parents and thereby slowly pushed the frontier of agriculture further on.

This model explains very well why a group of languages that seems to have its origin in a single language may have spread over an enormous expanse. Therefore, Renfrew's proposal is attractive. At the same time, it raises many questions that are far from resolved. There is an ongoing, quite vigorous debate among archaeologists and historical linguists on these issues.

At any rate, the Indo-European languages seem to have spread over large parts of the world at some time during the last 10,000 years. The next question is how other large language groups came into being. Before an answer is attempted, we will take a look at another interesting case, that of the Bantu languages in Africa south of the Sahara.

BANTU LANGUAGES

Keeping livestock and growing crops started much later in Africa south of the Sahara than in Europe. Up to about 3,000 years ago, central and southern Africa were peopled by scattered groups of gatherers and hunters, about whose languages we know little. Since that time, speakers of languages belonging to one group, the Bantu languages, have populated almost the entire continent south of the Equator.

The original speakers of Bantu languages may have been a comparatively small group. They first moved, or spread, from an original habitat in the west, perhaps somewhere in Cameroon, several thousand kilometres eastward to the shores of Lake Victoria. They acquired knowledge about farming and livestock, probably from the north, around 2,500 years ago. Later on there was a massive expansion down the continent, towards the south and south-west. The Bantu colonizers practised farming, and they probably became more numerous than the original inhabitants within a few generations in the areas where they settled.

At present there are about 180 million speakers of Bantu languages. They inhabit a very large area, more than 5,000 kilometres from north to south and around 3,000 kilometres from

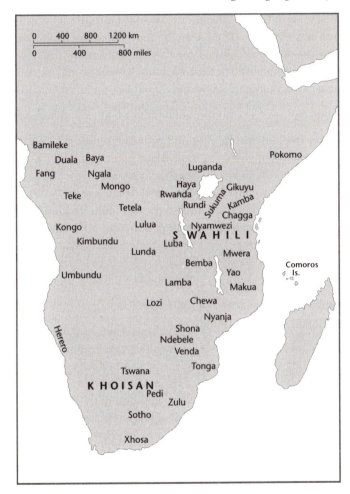

Map 2. The Bantu languages

east to west. It seems that they replenished this part of earth in the way Renfrew thinks that the Indo-Europeans took over Europe; through growth of population when farming and livestock were introduced. Renfrew himself has pointed out that this parallel supports his theory.

But there are also differences. The Bantu people and the Bantu languages seem to have spread much faster than the Indo-Europeans and their language did. At the same time, their original language has been fragmented to a larger extent. There are now around 100 Indo-European languages, many of which have large numbers of speakers. The Bantu languages are between 300 and 600! Only a few, such as Swahili, Zulu, or Xhosa, are known by name to people outside Africa. Most of the languages are spoken by few people; many of them have no written form and are not used in schools.

WHAT IS A BANTU LANGUAGE LIKE?

Languages come in very different shapes, but it is also true that all languages have much in common. All languages have words, consisting of sounds, the sounds are vowels and consonants, and the words are combined into sentences. Much else may vary. Most speakers of English either know no other language or know one or a few Indo-European languages, such as French, Spanish, German, or Latin. This is why it is easy to believe that features typical for our large language group are found in all languages of the world. A small sample of a language from another group, such as the Bantu languages, may be of some interest.

The language Setswana is spoken in Botswana and northern South Africa. Because writing was imported from Europe in the nineteenth century, the language is written in our Latin script, just as other African languages are south of the Sahara.

In Setswana, the word for "person" is *motho*, and "persons" is *batho* (*th* is pronounced as English *t*). "Girl" is *mosetsana*, and "girls" is *basetsana*. "Teacher" is *moruti*, and "teachers" *baruti*.

It can be seen that the words begin in *mo-* when only one is meant, but in *ba-* when the word is plural. Comparing with English and other Indo-European languages, one can see both a similarity and a difference. What is similar is that we too have different forms, like *girl* versus *girls*. The difference is that our language shows the distinction at the end of the words but in Setswana and other Bantu languages, the words begin differently.

This is one of the typical features of Bantu languages. The general principle is that singular and plural are expressed by different markers that are prefixed to the word stem. As we have seen, the singular prefix *mo-* and the plural prefix *ba-* are used with some stems. But there are other possibilities too. A slightly larger set of nouns is shown at Table 2.6. It can be seen that there are two classes of noun, one containing words for human beings that has *mo-* for the singular, *ba-* for the plural, and one containing other words that has *se-* for the singular, *di-* for the plural. There are more classes but this is sufficient to grasp the general idea.

The word for "school" is a loan from English *school*, which can be seen easily in the singular form. But there is an extra *e* at the beginning, since Setswana does not allow the sound sequence *sk*. That is why the word begins in *se-*, which happens

TABLE 2.6. *Singular and plural forms in Setswana*

Meaning	Singular	Plural
person	motho	batho
girl	mosetsana	basetsana
teacher	moruti	baruti
thing	selo	dilo
tree	setlhare	ditlhare
school	sekole	dikole

to be one of the normal prefixes for singular, as we have just seen. In the plural, the word then needs the prefix *di-*. And that is why the word for "schools" is *dikole*.

Adapting an English word to a Bantu language may not be easy, as is shown by the example. To introduce a Bantu word into English may also be tricky, as can be seen in the case of language names. The languages Swahili, Zulu, and Xhosa were mentioned above. As a matter of fact, these are not the names of the languages used in the languages themselves, for the English forms do not include the singular prefix that is obligatory for all nouns in Bantu languages. The names of the languages in the respective languages are Kiswahili, Isizulu, and Isixhosa, forms that are sometimes also used in English. As for Setswana, it does include the prefix, but the form Tswana is also found in English.

So much for nouns and their inflection in Bantu languages. Of course this is just one of the features in their grammars, but a pretty important one. After this little digression, let us return to the main theme and finish the discussion about language groups.

OTHER LANGUAGE GROUPS

There are between 5,000 and 7,000 languages in the world at present, according to the best estimates. However, most people on earth speak one of the 100 to 200 large languages. Many of them have become large fairly recently. For example, English, Spanish, and Portuguese, originally European languages, are now spoken by several hundred million people in America. If one wants to know how languages spread a long time ago one has to consider the many original languages, usually small ones.

The picture is varied and rather confusing. There are many single small (and some large) languages in the world that are not related to any other language. They are usually called isolates.

The most well-known isolate is Japanese, a very important language with a long history of writing and with more than 100 million speakers at present. It is true that it has been suggested that the language is affiliated with other groups; Altaic and Korean are prime candidates. But there is no very solid proof for any such connection.

Another well-known example is Basque, which is used in northern Spain and south-west France, and is completely surrounded by Indo-European languages. It is certain that the language was spoken there when the Romans expanded over the area 2,000 years ago. Its previous history is unknown. But there are many such isolates over the world. Probably each one of them has a very long history of its own, but in most cases nobody knows anything at all about it.

However, most languages belong to some group, or language family, as the usual term is. The word "family" implies an analogy that is, in my view, somewhat misleading; languages may be similar for a number of reasons, and the relations between languages are not at all like human kinship. For that reason, the more neutral "language group" is used here.

The Indo-European and the Bantu languages seem to have arisen by spread from one original language for each of the groups; in such cases it is customary to talk about a parent language and daughter languages. Note that the "daughters" have only one "parent." In many other cases the situation is somewhat different. It is not unusual to find a group of languages that clearly belong together as they have similar grammars, similar sound systems, and partly common vocabulary, but for which it is very hard to reconstruct a common proto-language. This is the case with Semitic languages, for example. The reason may be that there have been a number of dialects or closely related languages that have influenced each other through continuous contacts for a very long time. In such situations, it may be impossible or pointless to posit relations of "daughter" and "parent."

Among the numerous language groups in the world, Indo-European and Bantu languages are not the only examples of significant spread during a relatively short period.

The Fertile Crescent, which is in Renfrew's view the starting-point for Indo-European languages, is also an area where speakers of Semitic languages are found. The oldest attested one of that group, Akkadian, was spread from the Mediterranean to the Persian Gulf more than 4,000 years ago. Around AD 1, Semitic languages were spoken in the Near East from present-day southern Turkey down to Yemen, and in Eritrea and Ethiopia in

Africa. How this came about is not very clear. The Semitic languages may well have spread from Africa to Asia a very long time ago, since the Semitic group is considered to be a subgroup of the Afro-Asiatic languages, and all the other branches of that group are found in Africa.

Sometimes the related languages are found at great distances from each other. The most famous example is that of the Austronesian group, which is found mainly on a large number of islands, from Madagascar close to eastern Africa via the large Indonesian islands, such as Borneo and Sumatra, through to New Zealand, Hawaii, and Easter Island. Clearly, the reason for this must have been migrations across the sea in the past.

The Uralic languages provide another example. To this group belong a number of languages in northern Europe; the largest ones are Finnish and Estonian. Hungarian, spoken in Hungary in eastern central Europe, is also a member of the group. A number of scattered languages are found in the eastern part of European Russia, and others far eastward in Siberia. Those areas are separated by thousands of kilometres; they are completely surrounded by Indo-European languages. Why this is so is not clear from recorded history. It is believed that the situation is a result of a complicated series of migrations, but most of these are not actually attested by any other evidence than the linguistic situation.

Most language groups, however, are geographically fairly coherent. A few examples of well-known groups should be mentioned. The one with the largest number of speakers is the Sino-Tibetan group. Chinese, with around 1,000 million speakers, is completely dominant in terms of speakers. But the group comprises almost 300 other languages, most of which are spoken by fairly few people. All the languages are found in eastern Asia, mostly more or less adjacent to each other, although Chinese is nowadays spread over a large part of the world because of extensive migration in the last centuries.

In most other large groups, no single language dominates to that extent. However, in the groups with a large number of speakers there are mostly a few languages with very many speakers, while most languages have few speakers. For example, the Dravidian group, found mostly in southern India, has four large languages (Tamil, Telugu, Malayalam, and Kannada) with more than 150 million speakers between them, and an additional 65 languages or dialects that share the remaining 9 million or so.

All in all there are around twenty large language groups that are generally recognized by linguists. There is considerable discussion about some parts of this classification. This is partly because many languages have not been studied very much, and partly because linguists do not always agree on the criteria needed to postulate a valid group. For example, most scholars think that there are a number of unrelated groups of American Indian languages in South America, but a few linguists believe that they all belong to one group, or "phylum," together with most languages in Central and North America.

However, no one questions the general picture that there are now a fairly small number of large language groups to which most languages belong, and then a number of isolates. The number of isolates is also much debated, as it depends very much on the criteria for inclusion in a group. From the historical point of view, this is of minor importance, as the general picture is clear.

Most languages belong to related groups which have spread over large areas. The central question of this chapter is how and why these groups formed and spread.

HOW LANGUAGE GROUPS WERE FORMED

The Indo-European languages and the Bantu languages have been discussed above. In both cases, a group of languages prevailed over large parts of the world some thousands of years ago. Was this diffusion of languages connected with some special period in the history of mankind? Much speaks in favour of that idea, and I have pointed to the basic changes in mode of life connected with the introduction of farming and with the raising of livestock. Other changes in technology must also have played a role. The Austronesian languages have spread over enormous expanses of sea. For example, Malagasy, the language of Madagascar, is most closely related to the Ma'anyan languages on Borneo; the distance is something like 6,000 kilometres. Obviously, this could happen only when people had reliable boats and could sail.

Thus, we can be fairly certain that the language groups that are found at present are the result of movements of people or of cultural diffusion caused in the changes in lifestyle. As has been explained above, these changes have been quite radical during the last five to ten millennia, and that is one reason to assume that time-span for the spread of the language groups that are found now. There is also another very good reason to do this.

This is the nature of language change. Historical linguists apply quite subtle methods to find out whether different languages may have had a common prehistory, and these are the methods that are used to establish the existence of language groups. However, there are limits to how far back these methods can take us.

It is often possible to reconstruct important aspects of the language situation two or three thousand years ago from languages that are spoken now. If there are old written sources, as is the case for some Indo-European languages, it is possible to reconstruct about as far back again, from the time when they were written. For earlier periods very little is certain, and those who make statements about relationships between languages stretching further back than ten thousand years (some people do) should not be taken very seriously, for there is no way to know about such matters. This is because after such a long time almost all words in a language have either been replaced or have changed literally beyond recognition.

But how does one know that languages had not spread widely at earlier times? The answer is simple: one does not know. At any rate, the languages themselves do not provide much information about that.

Thus it is not known whether languages spread over large areas in the distant past. This is quite possible, for our species dispersed from Africa only 100,000 years ago or so, and this must have meant that humans expanded over large territories. Attempts have been made to find out something about the languages of that time by tracing back from the languages we know. An interesting fact is that some features of grammars and sound systems tend to be similar to some extent for languages from the same general area. But in my view at least, it is not possible to know whether this is because the languages have influenced each other for a very long time or because there is some very remote common origin.

Most historical linguists share this opinion, but not quite all. A few think that it is possible to establish the existence of very early proto-languages, such as Nostratic, that is supposed to have been the proto-language of Indo-European, Uralic, Afro-Asiatic, and more. Some even believe that one can reconstruct relationships among all languages on earth and retrieve actual words from the proto-language that they suppose was the origin of all other languages. For my part, I think that these ideas are not founded on actual facts, but on preconceived notions and wishful thinking. There may have been an original language, but its words cannot be reconstructed from existing languages.

So, even if once upon a time there were large language groups other than the ones we know of, they have disappeared because societies have changed their forms of speech so much that virtually no common elements are left. It is like what happens when the sea erodes a big rock so that it is eventually reduced to a large number of pebbles.

In the case of the Bantu languages, this process is already far advanced. After a period of perhaps 3,000 years there are several hundred languages, most of which are spoken by few people.

To summarize, during most of the many millennia before the beginning of history there existed in all probability only small languages. A few thousand years ago, when farming and other technological changes altered the lives of men, it happened (not necessarily for the first time) that a few languages spread rapidly so that people spoke the same language throughout large populated areas. How and why this came about can be guessed, but hardly known; it had to do with the spread of agriculture and/or other technological innovations. It seems that those large languages in most cases were fragmented and became many smaller ones, giving rise to the large groups of related languages that exist now. This, then, is the more general answer to the question that was raised in the beginning of this chapter concerning Germanic languages.

But there is a complication. Some languages have not been subjected to this kind of fragmentation. For example, the Indo-European group comprises fewer languages than the Bantu group, even though it seems to have formed much earlier. Some languages in the group have very many speakers. Such large languages, with millions or many millions of speakers have appeared in the last few millennia, and by no means just in the Indo-European group. Chinese, Japanese, Tamil, and others are obvious examples.

The following chapters will show how and why the large languages arose and held sway.

Chapter 3
Writing and the Egyptians

RIVER VALLEYS AND STATES

When people began to till the earth, it soon turned out that some areas were better suited for farming than others. The most fruitful soils were found in some river valleys, and around the Euphrates and the Tigris as well as along the Nile many people settled close to each other. In these valleys they learnt to regulate the water supply through irrigation canals and dams.

A person who wants to plough and sow a piece of land and then harvest it has to rely on some kind of societal order that prevents other people from taking the crop. Even more stability and security is necessary for people to invest in digging canals. A canal is made to water several plots of land for many years, and will be dug only by people who stand a good chance of being able to retain both land and canal for a considerable time.

Sure enough, stable and orderly societies appeared in the river valleys. Those are the oldest communities we know any details about, and that is because of an innovation, the most important of all the inventions of mankind—writing.

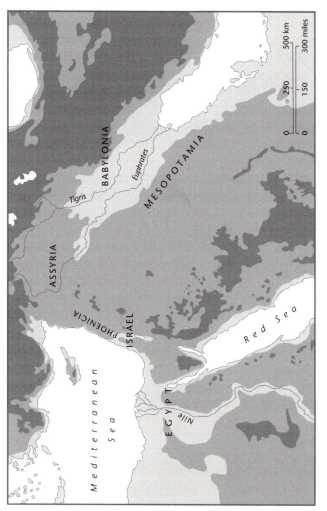

MAP 3. The civilizations of the river valleys

In the Euphrates and Tigris valley the Sumerians were the first to use what is known as cuneiform writing, starting around 5,200 years ago. After many centuries the Sumerians disappeared from the scene of history, and were succeeded by the Akkadians, and much later the Assyrians. All used the same type of script, although their languages were different. Cuneiform means "wedge-shaped," and the distinctive feature of this kind of writing is that the characters are formed by wedge-shaped marks on clay tablets.

The system was used continuously for 3,000 years, and was adapted to the requirements of about fifteen different languages. Still, many signs and basic features remained the same over the millennia, and Sumerian in fact lived on as a literary language for a very long time. It seems to have disappeared as a spoken language around 1800 or 1700 BC, but the scribes in Babylon in the sixth century BC still learnt to read and write Sumerian as well as their own language. Obviously, one of the important features of a script is that it can preserve old languages and language forms.

We shall concentrate here on a slightly younger script; we turn to the Nile valley and the Egyptian state.

THE STATE, THE LANGUAGE, AND THE SCRIPT

The first specimens of Egyptian writing are about 5,000 years old. At that time there already existed a strong, centralized Egyptian state that controlled the long, low, fertile part of the Nile valley with its large population. We know of this kingdom through the inscriptions in hieroglyphic writing, but also via thousands of monuments, works of art, and other archaeological remains. The Egyptian state under the Pharaohs surpasses all other political organizations in longevity. The Egyptian language was used officially in the state for around 2,700 years. Only after Alexander's conquest of Egypt in 332 BC was the language pushed into the background in favour of Greek, and not until 300 years later did Egypt cease to be an independent state.

As early as the first centuries of the kingdom, the Egyptians accomplished their most spectacular achievements by constructing the big pyramids. With the technology of that time, the building of one pyramid may have involved perhaps 100,000 people for decades. How was this possible?

A prerequisite was that all in this large realm could communicate with each other. This was simple if everyone spoke the same language, and that seems to have been the case, by and large. The Old Kingdom in Egypt may have been one of the first instances, if not the first, of hundreds of thousands or even millions of people using the same language. It meant, among other things, that representatives of the central power could travel to all parts of the country and make themselves understood.

The available information indicates that almost all inhabitants of Egypt spoke Egyptian, from oldest times up to the collapse of the kingdom 3,000 years later. Possibly one small language group had become much larger when agriculture was introduced. We cannot be certain what happened and why.

But what is really remarkable is that a large population kept talking the same language for thousands of years, and that it did not split up into dialects, which in turn developed into separate languages. This tells strongly against what is said above about languages being liable to change and split. The Egyptian language did change over time, as all languages do, but it did not break up into several languages; it remained a unit. Why was this so?

The answer is obvious enough. The political homogeneity and the need for communication throughout the country were the forces that prevented the language from falling apart. Those who inhabited the Kingdom of Egypt just had to stick to the Egyptian language. This country is the first instance of how a people speaking one language established a large state and dominated it for a long time. The language and the state became allies, as it were, mutually supporting each other.

To be sure, this is only part of the explanation. For if this were the whole truth, why do not all states with only one language remain intact for three millennia? To counter this, it would be necessary to discuss the traditionalistic culture of the Egyptians in more detail. But the general lesson is still valid. A strong state mostly has a dominant language, and the state supports that language. Languages depend on states, and states depend on languages.

But back to the question of how the Egyptians could manage the building of pyramids. In addition to a common language, there had to be a surplus of labour. When all necessary work had been done in the fields and in the canals, in order to ensure food for all, many people must have had time left to attend to other tasks.

That labour force had to be used for the pyramids, and other projects decided by the state. Therefore hundreds of thousands must have got food and lodging while they were building, without doing any farming of their own. In some way, then, the food had to be taken from the farmers and given to the builders. Or in other words, to maintain the construction work the state had to exact heavy taxes from the farmers. And that was indeed the case.

But taxation requires a system including delivery dates, checks, lists of taxes and taxpayers, and receipts. And what is needed for lists and receipts? A written language. An organization as complex as the one needed to construct a giant pyramid requires the use of writing.

Many believe that the need for taxes and receipts was the original impetus for the invention of writing. In the case of cuneiform writing, there was clearly a preliminary stage before the development of a complete writing system, when there were symbols for numbers and for goods that were used in lists and receipts, but no method for writing complete texts. But in the case of the hieroglyphs, even the earliest examples show a system that can be used to write down any kind of message.

HIEROGLYPHS

The Egyptian hieroglyphic script is often seen as writing by means of pictures. Many of the signs do indeed clearly depict something, and the meaning of the sign is often in some way connected with what is depicted. But there is no way to guess the sense of the text just by focusing on the depicted objects. As a matter of fact, most signs represent just sounds of the language, and others carry an abstract or grammatical meaning.

Still, the starting-point is indeed representation by pictures. Thus, the sign ☉ means "sun", and the sign 👁 means "face." But this method takes care only of a small part of the elements of a language. Other ways must be contrived for writing the remainder.

One important device was to use pictures of objects for abstract concepts. For instance, the sign ☉ may mean "day," the time when the sun is seen. This is not far-fetched, and in fact some languages employ the same word for both concepts: in Setswana, *letsatsi* means both "sun" and "day." In this way it was possible to express a large number of concepts that cannot be depicted.

Another stratagem was to use a picture for an activity. The sign △ clearly represents two legs with feet, but the meaning is "arrive." This kind of transfer of meanings made it possible to denote many verbs.

This is still not nearly enough to represent all the words and meanings of a spoken language. It is necessary to convey somehow the sounds of speech through vision, for in practice there is no way to communicate a natural human language without reference to the sounds in some contexts.

For that purpose the Egyptians employed their signs according to another principle. The sign ⌣, for example, has the primary meaning of "mouth," as is not hard to see. Now, the spoken form of the word "mouth" in Egyptian was just *r*. The sign for "mouth" could then be used also for another meaning, "against," which happened to have the same spoken form *r*. In other words, a sign would sometimes be employed for the sound of what is depicted rather than for the depicted object itself.

A short additional step from this is to combine signs representing different sounds to form new words. The word meaning "name" could be written � ⌇⌇⌇⌇ . The sounds represented by the two signs were *r* and *n*, and the word meaning "name" was *rn*. This principle could be employed for longer words too. The sign meaning "house" is ⌷ , and its sound value was *pr*. It could be combined with ⌒ , with the sound value of *t*, to form the word *prt* "winter."

The Egyptian words as transcribed here look very odd, being devoid of all vowels. The reason is that the Egyptian script normally did not include vowels at all, and so they are simply not known. One reason probably was that the language had few vowels, which may not have been very important for distinguishing between meanings. So we do not know if the word for "mouth" was pronounced *ra* or *ru* or perhaps *ar*, and if "name" was *ran* or *rin* or something similar. What one can be certain about is that there were vowels in Old Egyptian. It is not possible to speak a language without vowels, so they all have them.

Disregarding the vowels, the Egyptians were able to represent the sounds of any word with the help of their signs. The idea behind the representation of sound by pictures is sometimes called "the rebus principle," as a rebus is also based on the notion of combining pictures that represent parts of words.

The script was not always easy to interpret, as many signs may mean either what they depicted or the sound value of that word. This is why there were also explanatory signs, called determinatives. They were placed after a "spelt" word in order to show what kind of word was intended. The determinatives also started out as pictorial signs. The sign for "sun" was used also as a determinative for all words connected with light, time and seasons. Thus it was possible to write first the signs ⬚ ◠ and then add ⊙ to give the clue that this is a word having to do with time, in this case *prt* "winter."

All this may sound complicated; it is. Learning to read and write hieroglyphs was very time-consuming, and only a tiny portion of the population mastered the art. Experts estimate that perhaps one person out of every hundred could read and write in ancient Egypt.

Some of those who did possess this knowledge were people in the highest echelons of society, but most of them were the ones who made reading and writing their profession, the scribes or secretaries. They dealt with taxes, of course, but also with official correspondence and bookkeeping. There were many inscriptions, often glorifying the Pharaoh or other important people, and numerous sepulchral monuments. But beyond that, there were hardly any texts for the general public to read.

For that reason there is much that we do not know about the linguistic situation in Ancient Egypt. In order for us to know about previous epochs it is necessary that the knowledge has been transferred. The earliest Egyptians wrote down little about other things than the official business of the state, and other facts are hard to come by.

As few people mastered the written language, it seems improbable that it could have influenced speech to any large extent. In modern times, the written language quite often is perceived as a model, or even an ideal, for the spoken form to imitate, but in a society with so few readers this can hardly have been the case.

Egyptologists have shown that the spoken language must have changed very much in the course of the three millennia of the Kingdom. But the hieroglyphic writing remained more or less the same for a very long time. It was used without any major alterations from the middle of the third millennium BC up to around AD 400. It is true that other writing systems appeared during this time and were used in parallel, but the hieroglyphic one remained in use throughout. It was based on the spoken language at the time of its introduction.

Those who became scribes employing the traditional script in the first centuries AD first had to learn a very complex way of rendering a spoken language in writing. They also had to learn what the language sounded like several thousand years before their time; otherwise they were not able to spell the words in the correct, traditional way. Hieroglyphs were difficult even at the beginning, but in the late period the learning task must have been tremendous. The last scribes may have faced a challenge almost as great as that of modern Egyptologists.

WRITING SYSTEMS AND SOCIETY

There are other writing systems similar to the Egyptian one and the Sumerian one. The most important one still in use is the Chinese script. Such systems are often called logographic, meaning "word-writing," although as we have seen many characters actually stand for syllables or single speech sounds.

While the Egyptian system was probably created under some influence from the cuneiform script, the Chinese writing probably evolved quite independently. However, it is considerably younger; texts in Chinese first appear around 1200 BC. But by now, the script has been in use for more than 3,000 years, and is still very much alive; it is used by hundreds of millions of people.

This type of writing is by its nature more conservative than alphabets are. An alphabet conveys sounds, and as the sounds of a spoken language are always in a state of change the difference between written and spoken language constantly becomes larger. But it is possible to reform the spelling so that the direct connection between the spoken sound and the written symbol is restored.

In a script of a more symbolic kind some signs denote meanings without any relation to the pronunciation. Even those signs that principally denote sounds are connected with an object or a notion. That is, the signs do not convey only sounds but also another kind of content. For this reason, such a script is more liable to remain unchanged even if the spoken language is thoroughly transformed.

It may not be entirely accidental that two of the most long-lived and most conservative cultures in history, the Egyptian and the Chinese, have both employed symbolic writing systems. The very nature of the script may have contributed towards retention of norms, notions, and societal order.

However that may be, it is a fact that logographic writing systems have been in use for a very long time and that one of them is used now by a substantial part of humanity. Such systems have some drawbacks in comparison to alphabetic systems, but also some advantages. There is no reason to regard one of the systems as superior; mainly, they are just different.

It should also be mentioned that there are and have been several writing systems in which the most important level of representation is neither the word nor the sound, but the syllable. The most important of these is Japanese writing. It was developed from the Chinese system, and a large number of Chinese logograms are still used, together with the characters that denote syllables. This system too is quite viable and has been in use for a long time in an important culture.

In Western societies with alphabetical writing systems it is sometimes believed or even taken for granted that logographic and syllabic writing systems are inflexible or somehow antiquated, and that they will eventually be abandoned in favour of the alphabet. There does not seem to be any reason to believe that this will happen. The systems work very well, and they are perfectly adaptable to modern technology.

As for book printing, that art was practised in China for several hundred years before it was introduced in Europe. When it comes to computer technology, only alphabetic characters could be handled in the early days, but that time is long gone. At present, Chinese and Japanese are used much on the Internet, and the rate of growth is very high.

So there are no intrinsic reasons why logographic or syllabic writing systems should not dominate the world. As a matter of fact, though, the alphabetic system conquered Europe, and from there eventually spread over much of the globe. The next chapter is about the first language with an alphabet.

Chapter 4
Greek and the Greeks

LANGUAGE AND ALPHABET

> The Pleiads have left the sky, and
> the moon has vanished. It's midnight:
> the time for meeting is over.
> And me—I am lying, lonely.

This is an attempt to translate a poem written in Greek around 2,600 years ago. From the Greek text it is clear that the "me" of the poem is a woman. The author was Sappho, a poet living on the island of Lesbos, an independent state among innumerable other small Greek states.

Here, language is used for something we have not considered above, not to organize hunting parties or the digging of canals, and not to collect tax or to pay homage to rulers and gods. The text is an artfully expressed statement about human experience, one of the first lyric poems.

This book is not about poetry, but about the relations between languages and history. However, in the case of the Greeks artistic language provides one of the keys to history. The Greeks did not create an empire that produced a strong language and an important culture, as was the case with the Egyptians and almost all later cultural centres. On the contrary, the Greek literary language, Greek philosophy, and Greek art were created first, and later on this Greek culture came to dominate several important empires.

A basis for the remarkable history of the Greek language is the invention of the Greek alphabet. It was modelled after Semitic scripts, with the important improvement that not only consonants but also vowels are represented by independent letters.

The poet Sappho had access to an alphabetic script, invented for the Greek language just a couple of hundred years before her time. The Greek alphabet is very similar to the Latin one, which is the one used for English. In fact, the Latin alphabet is derived from a variant of the Greek one. The similarity is easy to observe. Here is the original poem, written in the Greek alphabet:

> ΔΕΔΥΚΕ ΜΕΝ Α ΣΕΛΑΝΝΑ
> ΚΑΙ ΠΛΗΙΑΔΕΣ. ΜΕΣΑΙ ΔΕ
> ΝΥΚΤΕΣ. ΠΑΡΑ Δ' ΕΡΧΕΤ' ΩΡΑ.
> ΕΓΩ ΔΕ ΜΟΝΑ ΚΑΤΕΥΔΩ.

And in the Latin alphabet:

> DEDUKE MEN A SELANNA
> KAI PLEIADES. MESAI DE
> NUKTES. PARA D' ERKHET' ORA.
> EGO DE MONA KATEUDO.

One of the many advantages of alphabetic script is that it gives an indication of poetic rhythm. Even a person without any knowledge of Greek can see that there are eight syllables in the first line. That is true for the subsequent lines too. The second, the fifth and the seventh syllables in each line are prominent. That rhythm is imitated in the translation above.

It can easily be seen that the Greek alphabet functions in the same way as the Latin one, in principle, and that many of the letters are identical, such as T and M and N. In most other cases the difference is just a matter of design, such as Δ that corresponds to D, and Γ that corresponds to G. The letters for the vowels I, E, A, and O look just as in the Latin alphabet, and were (originally) pronounced in Greek just as in Latin, Spanish, or Italian. The English way of pronouncing these letters is quite peculiar, from the point of view of speakers of other languages, and has to do with a change in the English language. There are some more complex differences between the Greek and the Latin alphabet, but they concern relatively minor issues and are not considered here.

The similarity between the Greek and the Latin alphabet is best seen when upper-case letters are used, as above. They represent the original letter-forms. Mathematicians and others sometimes use lower-case Greek letters in English texts. If the poem is written with those letters it looks rather different (in normal spelling, a number of accents and other diacritics would be added):

δεδυκε μεν α σελαννα
και πληιαδες. μεσαι δε
νυκτες. παρα δ' ερχετ' ωρα.
εγω δε μονα κατευδω.

The Greeks, then, had access to a script that could represent the meaning and also the pronunciation of the spoken language. In that way the writers could reproduce their own way of speaking to a reasonable extent, and the readers could decide the pronunciation of the author. Hieroglyphs and cuneiform script did not generally work in that way, nor did Linear B, a mainly syllabic writing system used for very early Greek. In addition, the alphabetic script was easier to learn than the earlier systems, and for that reason many more people than just a small group of professional scribes could employ written language.

Both aspects were important, but the most significant no doubt was that many people did learn to read and write. Even though only a fairly small part of the total population was involved, Greek culture still became a written culture to a much larger extent than any previous one. The early texts are by no means only official or formal ones such as laws, funerary inscriptions, and official history, but also literary works. The earliest ones are the great epic poems, the *Iliad* and the *Odyssey*, which are usually dated to around 700 BC, but soon after that several other kinds of writing appeared. Sappho and others wrote lyric poetry in the seventh century BC.

Around the same time Greeks started writing about science and philosophy. In the early period they were much influenced by the high cultures in Western Asia and by Egypt, a fact that did not fit well with the idea of European superiority that grew strong in the mid-nineteenth century and was therefore for a long time played down or denied outright. However, they did advance beyond their predecessors, and as time went by they attained a standard that has in some respects never been surpassed. Authors such as Plato and Aristotle, who wrote their works in the fourth century BC, still wield an enormous influence both indirectly through all their followers and directly as they are still read by many.

LANGUAGE AS CREATION

Due to the very fact that poets, philosophers, and scientists used Greek, the language itself changed. The person who thinks in a new way is quite often in need of a new expression, a combination of words that did not exist before, or even a new word. Greeks had a large number of new ideas, and as a consequence many new words were created. Since they made use of the alphabet for reading and writing, the new words were recorded and preserved. In that way the Greek language was enriched by a large number of words and meanings that had not existed earlier in any language. The authors did not only create their own texts, they also contributed to making the language richer and more versatile.

Writing is not a necessary condition for advanced thinking. Socrates wrote nothing, but was still regarded by many contemporaries as the best of all philosophers. It is not unimportant, though, that Socrates did read his predecessors and adversaries in philosophy. Besides, we would know nothing about him and his ideas, had not Plato portrayed him in his writings. As it is, Plato and Aristotle are still read—not just because they were writers, for thousands after them have written much and are now forgotten. But the fact that they wrote was necessary for their thoughts to survive.

The written Greek language, created through the efforts of these and other writers, included many words that have become part of Western tradition; those words and concepts are still with us, in English as well as in other European languages.

We go to school and learn history (*historia* in Greek), mathematics (*mathematike*) and physics (*phusike*), and we may move on to geography (*geographia*) and philosophy (*philosophia*). We can devote ourselves to politics (*politike*) as we live in a democracy (*demokratia*), we may be engaged in our private economy (*oikonomia*) or pursue our esthetical (*aisthetika*) interests, such as theatre (*theatron*) or music (*mousike*).

In English and the other European languages there are clearly a large number of loanwords from ancient Greek. There are loans from many other languages too, but the Greek ones are special. Many of them help to structure our existence by providing the categories (*kategoriai*) into which we group the phenomena (*phainomena*) of reality. The Greeks partly created our way of understanding the world, and what they created lives on in our language.

ARE LANGUAGES EQUAL?

If Greek became such an important and truly outstanding language, was it then better than other languages or than it had been some centuries before? If so, how much better and in what ways? Can languages evolve as well as change? Is there a ranking order for languages, and if there is, what is it based on?

These questions are not exactly new. Ever since antiquity, people have had ideas about the relative worth of languages. Before the twentieth century most people actually took it for granted that such a ranking order exists, but the criteria for ranking varied. Some pointed to such facts as have been discussed above, an important literature and a rich vocabulary. Others have thought it more important that a language is associated with a powerful empire and is used by many people. For a long time the question was seen as belonging to the sphere of religion, and discussion centred on which was the original language, spoken before the confusion of tongues in Babel. On that count, Hebrew won most of the votes (but not all).

A recurrent idea was that some languages are civilized and developed, while others are barbarian and primitive, and this line of thought became dominant in Europe during the nineteenth century, the era of colonialism. The languages of the colonialists, such as English and French, were of course seen as developed by definition, while the languages used by the natives of the colonies were mostly classified as primitive.

In the early part of the twentieth century, many linguists and others, for example the prominent American anthropologist Franz Boas, attacked these ideas, for the good reason that they were contrary to fact. The languages spoken by "primitive" peoples such as the Indians in North America, the Bushmen in southern Africa, or the Aborigines in Australia turned out not to be primitive at all, in any reasonable sense of the word. They may have more complex syntax, more intricate morphology, and more difficult sound systems than any "developed" European language. As for the potential to express new thoughts and to form new concepts, that is inherent in the basic structure common to all human languages.

So there are no "primitive" languages, in the sense of languages not being suited for advanced thoughts and subtle distinctions. All languages are capable of being used for such purposes. It is true that there are differences in what has to be included in an utterance for grammatical reasons and what may be left out. Languages may also map reality in very diverse ways through their different sets of concepts. Therefore it is not necessarily true that everything that can be said in one language is also possible to say in another one. But there is absolutely no evidence that Greek, or Hebrew, or English, are particularly well suited for advanced thinking because of qualities they have and other languages lack.

Modern linguists generally draw the conclusion that all languages are of equal value. In many contexts this is the only reasonable view, particularly if one happens to believe that all humans are of equal worth. Every language is the native tongue of some people, and for every human being the first language is an important part of the personal identity. So to say that one language is of less value than another one is to degrade some people to a certain extent. Each language can be a fully adequate first language for its speakers, and has to be respected accordingly.

But everyone knows that people have varying capacities, talents, and fortunes, even if their value is equal. It is the same with languages. Potentially, Plato and Aristotle might have used any language, but as it happened they used Greek. A language can expand and be made a more versatile tool than before. In unfortunate circumstances it may also lose functions and become more restricted.

Every language is unique and has the same value as other languages, but languages are not able to express everything equally well. Potentially, all languages can fulfil all functions and express all thoughts, but it is not true that every language can do that in all situations. Languages are like men in that not all can do everything.

This matter was brought up previously, in the context of the vocabulary of San languages. It was pointed out there that the words in a language are the ones that are needed in the culture where the language is in use. When words are created in one language, and are then taken over in many other languages, as has been the case with so many Greek words, this means that elements of the original culture are transmitted, and often also transformed. The usual term for such transmitted words is loanwords. Actually, it is misleading: the words will never be returned to the donor, and when the transmission is complete they become integral parts of the new language and the new culture.

Is this good? There are different opinions. Many people think that their own language and their own culture should be protected from outside influence as much as possible. There is something to this, of course. Each language is a unique creation, and if it absorbs elements from another language, it becomes more similar to that one, and to that extent less unique.

But this line of reasoning is misleading, in my opinion. If a new word is introduced in a language, that makes the language richer and more functional. If it completely replaces an old word with exactly the same meaning, the language has not gained anything; but that is a rare case. Mostly, new words add to the functionality of the language.

In sum, then, all languages have the same unlimited potential, but some languages have better means of expression than others because of the vocabulary. Words can be taken over from one language to another without much difficulty, and that is a major way for languages to enhance their resources. In the case of the Greek language, it has served as a donor to an exceptional extent, to the benefit of all the languages at the receiving end.

Now, let us return to other aspects of Greek.

ALPHABET AND DIALECT

A writing system that reflects pronunciation can make life easier for readers and writers. But one consequence of such a system is that if writers speak different dialects they also write differently, provided there are no established conventions for how to write and spell.

During the first centuries of writing in Greek, both spelling and other features varied a great deal. It is not true that each author follows his or her personal whim, but each one writes in his or her own dialect.

In Greece at this time there were several quite distinctive dialects, which were, however, all mutually intelligible. The early literary texts were based on a number of dialects. Sappho, who came from Lesbos, wrote in the Aeolic dialect, while Plato, who lived in Athens in Attica, wrote in the Attic dialect.

From our perspective this is rather remarkable. It is true that there are authors writing in English who use local dialects for literary purposes. However, this is rarely done throughout, but mostly in dialogues, or possibly in a poem or a short story. And everyone is supposed to write the standard language in all other contexts.

But in early Greece there was no standard language. There were no school authorities, publishers, or anyone else who decided what was correct Greek. There could not be, as Greece was in no way a political unit. Those who spoke Greek lived in a large number of small independent states, and no state had sovereignty over the others.

Still there was a sense of belonging together among those who called themselves Hellenes, the name still used by the Greeks of today to denote themselves. (That we use the term Greeks more often than Hellenes is because we have taken up the word used by the Romans.) The ones who counted as Hellenes were the ones who knew about the Greek gods and heroes, who consulted the oracle at Delphi, who participated in the Olympic games, and who spoke the Greek language, *hellenike glossa*. The others were *barbaroi*, "barbarians," a Greek word for those who speak unintelligibly. Possibly the word imitates the sound: people who speak a foreign tongue may sound as if they are saying "bar-bar-bar."

So a uniform language and a single state are not necessary conditions for people to feel that they belong together. Nor is mutual peace, unfortunately. The Greek states fought frequently against each other and collaborated only a few times to fight a common external enemy. But the wars did not prevent them from reading each other's writers, and even learning each other's dialects.

The differences between dialects were easy to hear but still not always very large. For example, the word for "moon" in Sappho's poem is *selanna*, while the form in the Attic dialect is *selene*. Sappho wrote *mona* for "alone" (in the feminine form), which is *mone* in Attic. It can be seen that there is a systematic difference, in that the Attic dialect has *e* as a final vowel in many cases when the Aeolic dialect has *a*. Such things are not too hard to learn. What is remarkable is that writers sometimes actually learned to write in dialect different from their own. For example, a tradition developed that songs performed by choirs should be presented in the Doric dialect, and so Attic and other authors wrote their lyrics for choirs in Doric. This led to an extraordinary situation in the famous Greek tragedies, written by Aeschylus, Sophocles, and Euripides. All three were Athenians and wrote their plays mainly in Attic. But in the numerous songs and recitations for the choir, they use the Doric dialect (or an approximation to it). So the same author changes from one dialect to another time and again within the same work.

The Greeks created a common written language, which was still not uniform but had several written dialectal variants. In the Greek environment, where each state (*polis* in Greek) pursued its own political interests it was natural that the language forms of different areas were equal in prestige and usability.

But circumstances changed, as they always will.

FROM CITY STATES TO EMPIRE

In the course of the fifth century BC, Athens grew more and more powerful, at the expense of most other Greek states. The dialect of Athens, Attic, also gained prestige. Towards the end of the century, however, Athens lost much of its political clout. But the great change of scene took place seventy years later, in the 330s BC.

The Macedonians, who lived in what is now northern Greece, expanded their empire very fast. They subdued the whole of Greece and also all the countries around the eastern part of the Mediterranean, from Turkey through to Egypt, and in addition lands to the east, modern Iraq, Iran, and for a time even Afghanistan. They reached as far as the river Indus, the border of India, on their campaigns.

The Macedonians were not Greek, but had a language of their own, about which we know next to nothing. However, their leading class was deeply influenced by Greek culture, and their famous king, Alexander, had received a Greek education like many prominent Macedonians. His teacher was Aristotle, the famous philosopher. Alexander and his generals introduced Greek as the language of administration throughout their enormous realm.

After Alexander's death, the empire soon disintegrated. Egypt became the kernel of one state, a large swathe of land from present-day Turkey to Iran became another one, and Macedonia with Greece a third state. But Greek remained the official language in all three countries, and the military and administrative élite spoke Greek.

The type of Greek that was in use was more or less the Attic dialect. By and by, a slightly modified form of Attic established itself as the common written language in the whole region. It was called *koine*, meaning "the common (language)."

As this standard established itself as the official language of administration, it gradually ousted the traditional dialects. The dialects disappeared from written records after a few centuries, and it seems that they also ceased to be spoken.

In this way Greek changed from a language with several written forms for dialects in various states to a uniform official language for several large powers. Most people in those countries did not speak Greek at all, at least not to begin with. It could be said that Greek was used as a colonial language, more or less as English is in India and in various African states.

Greek had a very long history as an official language, although the states involved went through several transformations. Little more than a century after the conquests of Alexander, the Roman Empire began to make its influence felt around the eastern Mediterranean. After a determined expansion that lasted for a couple of centuries, the Romans finally integrated all the countries from Greece through to Egypt into their empire in the last century BC.

In the west, the Romans systematically propagated their language in the countries they conquered, but this was not their policy in the east. Greek was kept as the language of administration and power during the long Roman period. The Roman Empire had two official languages, Latin only in the west and mainly Greek (but Latin in a few contexts) in the east.

In the Roman period, the Greek language took on another very important role, that of the first written language of Christianity. Jesus spoke Aramaic, but the central Christian texts, which have been assembled to form the New Testament, are written in Greek, and Greek has remained the most important language for many Christians. However, early Christianity was not restricted to the use of that language only. In the west, the language of the church was Latin, as will be discussed later on. In the east many early communities used their own languages, among others Armenian, Syrian, and Coptic, and the important texts were translated into those languages.

The difference in language of administration, as well as in history, between the eastern and the western parts of the Roman Empire was certainly one of the reasons why the empire finally split in two. In AD 330, somewhat more than 300 years after the final conquest of the east, the emperor Constantine consecrated the city of Constantinople by the Bosporus and made it a second capital, equal to Rome. In the year 395, the Roman Empire was finally divided into a western and an eastern part, and the eastern one, which had Constantinople as its capital, soon used only Greek as a written language.

Constantine also did much for the Greek language in another way, for in effect he made the Christian faith the official religion of the empire. Before, it had been a religious sect among many others in the world of late antiquity. Greek was the language of the Church in the eastern part of the empire.

The area ruled by Constantinople, also called the Byzantine Empire, was quite large in the early period, and it persisted for a very long time. Its size diminished, mainly because of the increase of Muslim powers, but Constantinople remained the seat of the emperor up to the final victory of the Turks in 1453. Throughout the empire the official written language was Greek, used largely in the same way as *koine* in antiquity. Thus it was in use without interruption from Alexander the Great to the mid-fifteenth century, that is for more than 1,700 years.

THE NEW GREEK

The history of the Greek language does not end there; people did not stop speaking the language when Constantinople was taken. In Greece, the Greek language continued to be the spoken language even when the country was a part of the Ottoman Empire, from the fifteenth through to the eighteenth century. At the beginning of the nineteenth century Greece became an independent state, and the Greek language once more emerged as a written, official language.

But at this time it was no longer possible to resurrect the old written language and start using it as before. The spoken language had diverged so much from what was used in antiquity and in the Byzantine Empire that it was hardly realistic to use the old written form. Also, the new state was in no way a successor of the old empire. In the course of the nineteenth century, there appeared in its place two competing written languages. One is called *dimotiki*, "the popular (language)", and is reasonably close to modern spoken Greek. The other one, called *kathareuousa*, "the purified (language)" includes many more words and forms from classical Greek.

The two forms were rivals for a long time in literature, in the schools, and in official life. The language question was at times quite poisoned, and often politically loaded. *Kathareuousa* was associated with conservative views, and *dimotiki* with radical opinions. The last days of glory for *kathareuousa* (so far, at least) were the period of the military junta. *Kathareuousa* was decreed the obligatory language of schools in 1967, but soon after the fall of the junta, in 1976, *dimotiki* became the sole official language form. Not only *kathareuousa* but also *dimotiki* has much in common with ancient Greek, from which it originates, and it is written with the same alphabet that was introduced in antiquity, more than two and a half millennia ago.

There is an interesting difference between the Greek name for their language and the name used by others. In English one talks about "Modern Greek," separating this language from ancient and Byzantine Greek. In the same way, the French term is "grec moderne," the German "Neugriechisch," and so on. But the Greeks themselves, who speak and write the language, normally use the term "elliniki glossa," the Hellenic language, which is what the language was called in the time of Plato, 2,400 years ago. Naturally everyone is aware of the fact that the modern language is not identical to the ancient one, but the use of the same name shows the Greeks' strong sense of continuity.

LEARNING FROM THE GREEKS

The long and remarkable history of the Greek language almost completes a full circle. At first, the language was used mainly in present-day Greece. Later it became the language of the state all around the eastern Mediterranean, and remained so for more than a millennium. It disappeared again in most of the area, and for several centuries it was reduced to a tongue spoken by peasants in a corner of an empire using another main language. It gained vitality anew and is now an official language in the same region where it first appeared 3,000 years ago.

This tells a few things about what the histories of languages may look like. First, they are like all other history in that there is no way of telling what will happen in the long run. If anyone had predicted, in the year 400 BC, that Greek would become the official language of half the known world 100 years later he would have been rightly regarded as mad. Still, just that happened. In that way, the fortunes of languages are no different from the fortunes of states.

More specifically, one should note how dialects developed. It has been explained above that variations always arise in a large language area, so that dialects emerge. It was mentioned that the various Germanic languages, for example, arose through the splintering of an original language into dialects, which later became separate languages as they drifted further and further from each other. There have been several developments of this kind, and they are particularly well documented within the Indo-European language group. Sometimes this is seen as a typical or even inevitable process.

But the history of Greek demonstrates that this is not necessarily so. In very old times, more than 2,000 years ago, there were several clearly distinct Greek dialects that also had written forms of their own. They did not diverge and develop into languages of their own; instead, something entirely different happened. A common form of speech and writing was established, and it became so strong that it almost entirely eliminated the other dialects. They disappeared as written languages, and evidently as spoken forms too. Modern Greek has dialects, to be sure, but they have developed from the common form, *koine*, and are not related to the ancient dialects of Aeolic, Doric, and so on.

There is one interesting exception. In a few villages in the Peloponnese people speak Tsakonian, a language that is not understood by other Greeks and seems to stem from the ancient Doric dialect. This shows that if the old dialects had lived on they would most certainly have developed into languages of their own. But as a succession of strong empires used a dominant form of the language, the original dialects were all but annihilated.

So there is no law of nature stating that languages have to split up into dialects that then become languages of their own. If people move apart and if they are not politically united a split will probably occur after some time. But if there is a common state and the state favours one particular form of the language the other dialects may be weakened and disappear.

A common written language definitely contributes to lessening dialectal differences, especially if the authority of a strong state supports it. The Greek example proves that a language may in fact exist in the same area for several thousand years without ever splitting. Something similar is true for Egypt, as was shown above, but we know much more about the dialectal situation in Greece, and that allows us to draw safer conclusions.

From the recent fight between the two written forms, *katha-reuousa* and *dimotiki,* it can be seen that language is connected with politics in another way too. An archaic and conservative written form was pitted against a more modern one, closer to the spoken language. The choice is by no means just a matter of linguistic preferences. It has a lot to do with one's attitudes to preservation and innovation in other spheres of life. Linguistic conservatism and political conservatism do not always coincide, but in Greece that was so, and there are several similar cases.

But the most important fact concerning the Greek language may be its role as the vehicle for Greek culture. Thoughts and ideas that remain fundamental for the Western tradition were first expressed in ancient Greek. The Greeks created several kinds of literature, such as epic and drama, and of course they wrote their literature in Greek. To read all this in the original form it was necessary, and still is necessary, to learn the language. Through its use in so many contexts the written form of the language developed into a more versatile and useful instrument for human activities than any system of writing had been previously, mainly because of the rich vocabulary and the large stock of existing texts of many kinds.

This was a major reason why the Macedonians chose Greek as the official language of their empire. The Romans, who were culturally very much under the influence of the Greeks from early times on, allowed their language to remain the official one for the eastern part of their empire; it had prestige because of its role in culture. Those in power could not introduce anything else to match it, but preferred to utilize it for their own purposes. Later on it attained even higher status, as it became the language of the first and most important texts of Christianity.

Throughout its history, Greek has had a cultural capital of its own which it has managed to retain throughout the rise and fall of several empires. In rare cases, a language can turn out to be stronger than political might.

Chapter 5
Latin and the Romans

Yours is the destiny, Roman, to rule over peoples and nations!

This verse brilliantly epitomizes the unbearable attitude of official Rome. It is found in a central passage in the *Aeneid*, the national epic of the Romans, written by Virgil at the instigation of the Emperor Augustus.

The verse has been used by imperialists of later times too. I own a copy of the *Aeneid* printed in Italy in the 1930s, during the era of Fascism. This very line is displayed prominently on the cover.

As an empire builder, Mussolini was a bungling amateur. But not only he but also much more competent conquerors of modern times, such as Napoleon, fade in comparison with the Romans. The Roman conquests were usually not as swift and spectacular as those of the Corsican, but they were much more durable. An important reason was their success in propagating their own language.

The earliest Rome was an insignificant city-state among a multitude of similar states in the middle of the Italian peninsula. According to tradition Rome was founded in 753 BC, and modern historians and archaeologists are inclined to think that this is not very far from the truth. In the first few centuries the state did not include much more than what is now the city of Rome. The Roman language, Latin, at that time was spoken only in Rome, even though some other small states in the vicinity probably used similar languages.

More or less from the beginning, the Romans had their minds set on capturing more land and subduing neighbour states, and their sphere of influence grew over the centuries. In the fourth century BC, they became the dominant power in the Italian peninsula, and towards the end of the following century they were the undisputed lords of Italy, including Sicily. They systematically expanded eastwards as well as westwards, and when the empire reached its maximal size, around AD 100, the Romans ruled over all Europe west of the Rhine (except Scotland and Ireland) and south of the Danube, all northern Africa including Egypt, and further present-day Palestine, Syria, Turkey, Greece, Albania, and a great deal more. Thus, the empire comprised everything around the Mediterranean and vast regions beyond that. This enormous power remained largely intact for another 300 years, until the fifth century AD, when the western part was dissolved through the invasion of German groups.

The Latin language is found in a few inscriptions from around 600 BC. As early as that there was a written form for this language, as well as for other languages in Italy. The Romans probably acquired the idea of a written language from their northern neighbours, the Etruscans, who constituted the dominating group in central Italy down to the fifth century BC. The Etruscans had adapted the Greek alphabet to the needs of their language, and the Romans in turn modified the Etruscan script to create the Latin alphabet, which has since then been used for about two and a half millennia by many peoples to write a large number of languages. It can still be seen almost everywhere, for example in this book.

From the centuries before around 300 BC, we have only a small number of inscriptions in Latin; no long texts have survived. In fact, the Romans were mainly farmers and soldiers and probably did not write a lot. From the end of the third century, however, Rome became a place with very large economic resources, a centre for trade in close contact with Greek-speaking cities around the Mediterranean, and at that time Latin was established as a literary language. In this field, as in others, the Romans closely followed Greek models to begin with.

Soon, however, Roman literature was prominent in its own right, and it reached its peak in the first century BC and the first century AD. Prose authors such as Cicero and Caesar, and poets such as Virgil and Horace produced works that are still read, and in the process they created a literary language and literary genres that have served as models for European writers during two thousand years.

But there are great differences between the origin of Greek writing and literature and the corresponding events in Rome. In the first place all Roman writers from the very beginning used one homogeneous language. There are no dialectal differences, for the written form is based upon the language spoken in Rome, as a matter of course. This reflects the fact that the Roman state was completely dependent on its centre, Rome, while all the rest was just a periphery.

Secondly, the Roman writers almost without exception lived in Rome, and they frequently belonged to the very uppermost layer of society. Cicero and Caesar both became leaders of the government, the historians Sallust and Tacitus were high military commanders and officials, and the philosopher Seneca was the guardian and teacher of the emperor, Nero. The poets Virgil and Horace were not powerful men, but the personal protégés of the emperor, Augustus. Men close to the very heart of power created much of Roman literature.

It might also be said, however, that those people occupied their dignified positions partly because they could write and speak so well. In Rome, it was a prerequisite for real success to be able to deliver persuasive speeches in front of large assemblies. The children of important people spent much time learning to speak in public; Roman education was largely rhetorical education. This meant, among other things, that pupils read much to enrich their language and that they had very systematic training in composing and delivering speeches. To master the Latin language in speech and writing was the key to success in Roman society.

This attention to language, not to say obsession with it, had as one of its consequences that the norm for correct language became very well established. Preferably, everyone should speak and write just like the best speakers and writers in Rome did. Masters of grammar and rhetoric taught and wrote down rules about almost everything: spelling and pronunciation, forms, choice of words, and levels of style.

In Rome, then, the power of the state was closely allied to a language, Latin, and to a very strictly defined form of that language. How far there were other forms, that is other dialects and other styles, we do not really know, as the preserved texts are totally dominated by the official form of the language. Here and there, in graffiti and in rare texts mimicking everyday speech, we can catch glimpses of the social variation that is bound to have existed. Not everyone can possibly have talked just as Cicero did. But there is no evidence that people in different parts of the empire developed dialects while the Roman rule lasted. By and large the Latin language as we know it varies little.

What did ordinary people actually speak in all the provinces outside Rome? In the beginning Latin was spoken only in the city itself, as was said above. With time Latin spread, both as a written and as a spoken language. It is hard to follow the details of this development, but the main facts are clear. A few hundred years BC there were several languages in Italy with more or less well-established written forms, and a few of them certainly had more speakers than Latin had. There are extant texts in Etruscan, Oscan, Umbrian, and others. Over the centuries the inscriptions and other texts in those languages become less and less frequent, and it seems that not one of them was used in writing after around AD 100. They may have been in use as spoken languages after that, but there are really no hints that this was so. At any rate they disappeared a very long time ago, almost certainly during antiquity. No modern languages are derived from them, so evidently Latin took their place in the whole of Italy.

In large parts of western Europe the same thing happened. Present-day France, Spain, and Portugal, as well as the islands of

Sicily and Sardinia, were inhabited by peoples speaking many languages when the Romans conquered these territories in the two last centuries BC. There is evidence that in late antiquity they had mostly shifted to Latin, and the overwhelming majority of the present population speak languages that stem from Latin. Only a couple of groups stick to other languages: the Basques in northern Spain and south-western France, and the Bretons in Brittany. But the Bretons are believed to be descendants of Celts who moved in from England in late antiquity, rather than a Celtic population who kept their language intact in Roman Gaul.

Latin remained a spoken language in other areas too, as in parts of Switzerland and in Romania.

How come that people shifted to Latin to such a large extent? The fact that a country is conquered and politically dominated by a state using another language does not necessarily mean that people abandon their original language, even in the long run, as was pointed out previously. For instance, Welsh is still a viable language in Wales, after 700 years of English rule. History presents a large number of similar examples, and so the massive language shift in the Roman Empire needs an explanation.

One reason is certainly to be found in the style of government. The Romans did devote themselves to spectacular conquests, but once they had occupied a territory they also worked hard on establishing an efficient administration. There appeared governors and soldiers, to be sure, but also tax collectors, judges, surveyors, customs officers, and many others. Commerce was largely put in the hands of Roman merchants, who were given preferential treatment.

In this situation, those who wished to advance in society, or just protect their position, had to learn Latin. It was necessary for almost any career, and mastery of the language entailed many advantages. Also, Rome was primarily a military power, keeping large numbers of soldiers in garrisons all over the empire. The language of the army was always Latin, so that those who chose that walk of life had to know the language. Many young men did so. The schools also used exclusively Latin (and Greek at more advanced stages).

People in towns probably shifted to Latin within a few generations, while those in the rural areas, who naturally constituted the majority, kept their original language much longer. But with time, Latin spread in the countryside, too. One reason why even the more resistant groups shifted in late antiquity may have been that Latin was so closely linked to the new religion, Christianity.

In Rome, Christianity arrived early. When the city burned in AD 64 the adherents of the new sect were accused of arson, and the emperor Nero sent many Christians to torture and death. The gospels and other Christian texts were translated from Greek to Latin at a very early period, and the Christians in the western part of the empire consistently used Latin in their churches. Christianity increased in strength and in the fourth century, after the conversion of Constantine, it became associated with the Roman state. The Church required participation and devotion on a scale quite different from any authority of the state.

In this way, the population of south-western Europe became speakers of Latin. In addition, Latin became well established in North Africa in present-day Algeria, Tunisia, and Libya, presumably almost as well as in Europe. But after a few centuries those countries were subjected to new conquerors, the Arabs. The Arabic language was supported by Arabic political power and the Islamic religion, and Latin in due time disappeared together with the Christian faith, to be substituted by Arabic and Islam. This is another example of how a strong political power, acting in concert with a popular and demanding religion, is able to bring large populations to abandon a language and take up another one.

In other parts of the empire Latin never prevailed. We have already mentioned the fact that the Romans used Greek as the official language in the eastern part of the empire. In England, Latin did not secure a foothold strong enough to let it survive the fall of the empire, perhaps because the country was captured late and is located far from Rome. Possibly few Romans felt any real urge to emigrate to this northern outpost. In the absence of close contacts and long-lasting local influence, no shift occurred.

LANGUAGE SHIFT AND LANGUAGE EXTINCTION

By the end of the western Roman Empire in the fifth century AD, most people in south-western Europe and North Africa spoke Latin; there were only insignificant remains of other languages left in the area. A thousand years before, when Rome had just been founded, the peoples in the same area surely spoke a large number of languages, perhaps more than 100, and no language had very many speakers.

Just as in old Egypt, there was a compact of sorts between state and language. But in Egypt the effect was only that the language did not split, while in the Roman Empire the language of the state expanded. The strong central power with all its means and devices induced large parts of the population to take up Latin as their first language.

Language shift is not unique or very unusual, but has occurred repeatedly throughout history. However, there are many changes of political power in history, and far from all of them have been accompanied by any language shift.

The basic reason why people are usually not inclined to change to another tongue is that language is not just an important tool for communication, but also the most important means of identifying one's group and oneself. The language a person learns from his parents forges a strong emotional bond with the ones who use that language. That is why people do not give up their native language except for very strong reasons.

Still people do sometimes take the leap. The causes are usually similar to the ones in ancient Rome: influence from a strong state and economic enticements, sometimes working in common with an official religion.

A long-range effect of the language shifts in the Roman Empire was that the number of languages diminished. As has been discussed already, this has been the main trend in world history for several millennia. The usual way for a language to disappear is what probably happened in Roman times, that the speakers gradually shift from one language to another. In the first stage, families become bilingual, and in a later generation, the children start with the new language instead of learning the original language first. Later still, people stop learning the original language at all.

Is this good or bad? The answer is not obvious. When a language disappears it means that a cultural achievement is lost for ever. The formation of a language with all its words and expressions, grammar and sounds is a process that takes hundreds or thousands of years. It is an ongoing, collective act of creation in which thousands or millions of people participate. Some experiences and ideas of all those people are embedded in the language, and when it disappears all this is irretrievably lost.

On the other hand, languages are no museum pieces. They are tools to be used by people, and when people shift to another tongue, it means that in their actual circumstances they prefer the new language as a tool for themselves and for their children. The reasons are often similar to the ones in the Roman Empire. Education and culture, religion, contacts with important people, job, money, and power are important matters for most people. All those things are easier to come by if you speak a rich and powerful language than if you are stuck with a small and poor one. That is why it is often to the advantage of the speakers to relinquish their native language.

Language shifts and extinction of languages are quite frequent in modern times, so we will return to the topic. However, the later history of Latin is an interesting example of the opposite process, the birth of new languages. This will be the topic of the following chapter. But before that, the continuing role of Latin in Europe will be discussed.

LATIN AS AN INTERNATIONAL LANGUAGE

In the fifth century, the western Roman Empire was invaded by a number of German peoples: Ostrogoths and Visigoths, Sueves and Vandals, Burgundians and Franks. Each group managed to seize power in a part of the empire, which literally fell into pieces. The last emperor in the west was deposed in 476.

This political upheaval did not bring about any important change in the linguistic situation, to begin with. People continued speaking Latin in the whole area where they had done so previously. The Germans, who probably were not very numerous, formed a powerful upper class, but the subjects did not embrace their languages. On the contrary, all those Germanic languages disappeared after some time, mostly without leaving many traces. It is true that Gothic was established as a written language, mainly through a translation of parts of the Bible that is still preserved in a manuscript from the fifth century, but as a spoken language, Gothic disappeared just like the languages of the other invaders. The only area where the invaders kept their language was Britain; this will be treated later. On the Continent, the Germans did not lose their power, but after some time the new generations shifted to the language of their subjects.

The reason was that the German conquest was very different from that of the Romans a number of centuries before. The Germans knew how to make war, but they had no administrators, tax collectors, merchants, road engineers or priests. There were no written forms of their languages that could replace Latin in legal and economic contexts. They could achieve a military takeover, but civilian life went on more or less as before.

In that way it might be said that Latin and Roman culture vanquished the Germanic intruders. But this was in no way a complete victory. Many things changed when the empire was dissolved into small kingdoms, and often enough into even smaller principalities and duchies. Communication and commerce were curtailed. The cities and towns lost most of their importance and were depopulated. In that process, the knowledge of how to read and write almost disappeared in many areas. Schools survived almost exclusively within monasteries and churches. The dominant economic pattern became self-subsistence, and in many areas the only political entity of any real importance was the local manor or estate. In the seventh century, western Europe was without any strong political power and well-nigh without any organization at all apart from the Christian Church.

This of course had important consequences for language. There is not much direct testimony, as people wrote little during these centuries, but it is possible all the same to make some informed guesses about what probably happened.

Whatever was produced in writing was in Latin. Even though the empire disappeared Latin remained the only written language within the old boundaries, and even beyond them, for a long time. Throughout the sixth century there was a comparatively large output in writing, and the authors had mostly learnt to write in the classical manner. In the seventh and eighth centuries very few texts were produced, and their language is often quite strange. The writers evidently wanted to write in the classical manner, but their lack of education made that impossible, and what they wrote down is sometimes not even comprehensible.

During these centuries something crucial must have happened to the spoken language. The previously strong influence from the central power of Rome had vanished. The army was not there any more, the schools had closed down, and no merchants carried ideas and expressions from one part of the empire to another. Each little nook was left to itself, and external contacts were reduced to a minimum. In a way this meant reverting to the situation before the conquests of Rome.

The consequences for language were the ones that might be expected. The various forms of speech in different parts of the old Roman Empire became more and more different. Each region developed its own speech habits. Latin had shown little or no dialectal variation while the empire lasted, but within a few centuries after that it was transformed into a multitude of regional and local dialects.

We know this because we can conclude it from what happened afterwards, and because there are some written reports about how people spoke in various parts of the former empire. However, no new written languages appeared for a long time. Those very few who wrote anything at all in the seventh and eighth centuries always used Latin, as best they could. Almost all of them were clergymen or monks.

Around 800 the situation changed. The schools of the Church were reformed and improved, and more and more people learnt to read and write Latin. By the twelfth century Latin was used very extensively in writing all over Europe, also in several countries that had never belonged to the Roman Empire, such as present-day Germany, Poland, and Denmark. It was the dominant written language everywhere, and in many countries no other language was written at all. Although it was by this time definitely no one's native language, Latin was also much used as a spoken language, particularly within the Church. Spoken and written Latin was taught in school.

For several centuries Latin remained the common written language of Europe. With time, competition from other written languages increased, but it held its own for long in most contexts. Only very slowly did it lose ground, as will be treated in more detail later on.

In the Church Latin prevailed up to the time of the reformation in the early sixteenth century, when the Protestant Churches introduced the national languages in church services. Within the Catholic Church, Latin was used longer than anywhere else. Up to the 1960s Latin was still spoken at the altars of Catholic churches all over the world.

In the world of science and higher education, Latin also remained a written and spoken language for a very long time. It only became acceptable to write scientific and scholarly texts in other languages as late as the eighteenth century. The great thinkers of the previous century, such as the Frenchman Descartes, the Englishman Newton, and the German Leibniz, all wrote their pioneering works in Latin.

Thus Latin did not disappear as a written language or as a learned language when it was no longer used as a first language by anyone. For many centuries it functioned as a written language for people with various native languages, and it was superseded only very slowly in a process that took many hundreds of years. It is still used to some extent both in the Catholic Church and in some areas of science, mainly as the language for international terms and names in medicine and biology.

For a long period, then, all educated Europeans (including Englishmen, of course) were at least bilingual. They had a native language, and in school they had learnt to write and speak Latin. In fact, that was what school was mostly about, which was of course a problem, as the pupils had little time for other subjects. On the other hand, when they had learnt Latin people were able to communicate with other people all over Europe, both in writing and speech. The language was truly international. In our time, English is taking on a similar role in large parts of the world, as will be discussed later. But so far at least, English is not nearly as well established as an international language as Latin was in Europe six or seven centuries ago.

The fact that the Latin language could reach this position in Europe had much to do with the standing of the Church. For many centuries the Christian faith was the dominant ideology, and the Christian Church was the dominant organization. From the very beginning the western Church had chosen Latin, and it persisted. The Church was responsible for most formal education during the better part of a millennium, and that was crucial. The authorities in charge of school curricula generally wield the real power when it comes to a choice of written language.

This shows that a society need not use a written language that is based upon what people speak. Written languages are learnt in schools by children who have already been able to speak for a long time. It is quite possible to learn a completely different language at that age, and never learn to write the first spoken language. That was the case in Europe during much of the Middle

Ages, and hundreds of millions of people today in Africa and Asia are in a similar situation.

LATIN: THE LANGUAGE FOR THE EUROPEAN UNION?

In the last few decades Europe has seen dramatic political change. The large countries, whose relations have shifted over the centuries between periods of balance of power and periods of war, have formed a union into which the smaller countries have also been allowed. Each state has one national language (or more), and each state insists on its right to use its language in all contexts within the Union. That is why all important documents are written in eleven languages, and business for interpreters and translators is better than at any time in history. In that situation some have proposed that it might be a better solution to resort to Latin, the old common language of Europe, as the linguistic tool of the Union.

As a matter of fact it would probably be possible. To be sure, it is unusual for a language to be revived after having disappeared as a spoken language long ago, but it has happened at least once. Hebrew vanished as a spoken language much earlier than Latin did, but in the course of the twentieth century it once more became a vital spoken and written language in Israel. The same could come to pass in the case of Latin.

However, it is easy to see the problems that would arise. Unless the big companies, the important universities, the diplomatic world, the international organizations, and so on all accepted a shift to Latin, the Union and its bureaucracy would become an isolated enclave. In practice everyone would have to learn English and French too, at least. Europe would train a special class of bureaucrats, with a high proficiency in Latin that could be used only for communicating with people they could more easily talk or write to in some other language.

So Latin is not the solution for the language problems of present-day Europe, nor is any other non-national language. The main advantage of Latin, of course, is precisely that it is not associated with any state (disregarding the Vatican). But a special language for the European Union makes sense only if the Union grows so strong that it can decide that all citizens in the member countries have to learn the language of the Union in school, rather than any other major language.

Nobody knows whether something of that kind may happen. But judging from world history so far, it seems much less improbable that some power inside or outside Europe will take control of the whole continent, thereby securing a dominant role for its own language. Had the Second World War ended in another way, something of that kind might have occurred half a century ago.

Be that as it may, Latin remains important as a language of Europe and the world, not because it is still used to some extent but because it has left its traces in all important European languages, including English.

THE INFLUENCE OF LATIN

As Latin was used so much and for so long all over Europe it has affected all main European languages. The languages of western

Europe have much of their vocabulary in common. This vocabulary consists mainly of Latin words, and of Greek words that were first taken up in Latin and then transmitted to the modern European languages. The English words have very often taken the route via French.

The verse from Virgil that introduced this chapter runs like this in Latin:

Tu regere imperio populos, Romane, memento!

A literal translation is: "You, Roman, remember to reign over the peoples in empire!" Each single word in the sentence forms the basis for one or more English word. *Regere*, "govern," is the origin of such English words as *regent* and *regiment*, and its participle, *rectus*, "governed," is at the base of words such as *correct* and *direct*. English "reign" is from a closely connected Latin word *regnare*. *Imperio* has yielded English "empire" as well as a number of other words, such as *imperialism* and *imperialist*. *Populos*, "peoples," has been introduced into English via French in the form *people*, but the same Latin word has also been a more direct model for such words as *population* and *populist*. *Romane*, "Roman," goes together with the name of the city, *Roma* in Latin. In English, there are also other words derived directly or indirectly from the name, such as *romance* and *Romania*. *Memento*, "remember!" is sometimes used without change in English, in the sense of "reminder." The root from which this word is formed is also found in such English words as *memory*, *memorize*, and *remember*.

In sum, each single word in the Latin verse is connected with several normal, ordinary English words. All are borrowed either directly from Latin, or through French, or more rarely via some other modern European language such as Italian. The exception is the first word in the verse, *Tu*. There is indeed an English (somewhat obsolete) counterpart, *thou*, but this is one of the cases of common heritage. Both the Latin and the English form have been inherited via their respective predecessors from Proto-Indo-European.

Latin has provided English with many of its words, through direct or indirect borrowings. The Latin words are more often abstract concepts than designations for common things, as can be seen from the examples. Latin and Greek have supplied both words and conceptual frames that can be used to describe and understand reality. Without concepts the world remains chaotic. On the other hand, concepts may attribute to reality a coherence that may not exist anywhere else than in the concepts themselves. For better or for worse, the European vocabulary, based on Latin and Greek, has provided us with the spectacles through which we can observe and discern the features of what exists.

Chapter 6
Did Dante Write in Italian?

HOW LANGUAGES BECOME LANGUAGES

Latin eventually disappeared as a spoken and a written language, and other languages took its place. How did this come about? Many have pondered the question, and there has been a considerable amount of research. Still it is not easy to say what happened, but not chiefly because it is sometimes difficult to establish the sequence of events. The main problem resides with the concept itself. When is something a language, and at which point does it become another language? And what is a language?

This last question was brought up earlier in connection with the Khoisan languages. When one first thinks about the problem its does not appear to be very complicated, but the more one tries, the trickier it becomes. Linguists and philosophers have been busy defining the concept of language for centuries, but they have not arrived at any very satisfactory solution. Or rather, everyone agrees nowadays that the term "language" is used in many different ways and that it denotes many different types of phenomena.

To begin with, I will try to clarify the issue with respect to spoken languages. All humans (excepting deaf people and some with other serious handicaps) speak at least one language. And there is no point in speaking a language only on your own, so each language is spoken by a group of people.

If there are only clearly delimited groups, and if each group uses its own language that is not similar to the language of any other group, there is no problem; but this is rarely the case. Very often groups of people speak similar languages, and quite often they can understand, more or less well, what people from other groups say. And what is a group? There is no very good answer to that question either.

This is why it is not possible to find the languages just by investigating the way people talk and finding out if they understand each other. Those are not the only factors that decide the existence of languages. Of course those facts are important, since usually people think that they speak the same language as the people they can understand, and that they do not speak the language of people they do not understand. But it is not always that simple. And one usually has to accept that the languages the speakers believe in are the ones that exist.

A clear example of this is found in Scandinavia. Swedes usually understand Norwegians very well, and Norwegians understand Swedes. Still Swedes and Norwegians agree wholly that Norwegian is one language, and Swedish is another, different language. By and large, they have also been able to persuade the rest of the world that this is the case. The decisive factor is what people think about their language, not how similar it is to another language.

The same thing must be true for situations in the past. Thus, Latin disappeared as a spoken language when people no longer thought that they spoke Latin. In other words, Latin disappeared not primarily because the language changed into something else, but because at some time the speakers decided to call the language something else.

Not all linguists would agree with this. Or rather, many people have not thought about the matter in those terms. At any rate, there are quite a few articles and books arguing that Latin changed into Spanish or French at some specific time because certain changes occurred at that time in the sound system or in the vocabulary.

But this way of looking at the problem is just plainly wrong. It is not possible to decide when a language changes to another one just by studying the sounds or the words or any other aspect of the linguistic system. It is a matter that is decided by the speakers themselves, not settled in any objective way. It would not be prudent to try to prove to a Swede that in reality he speaks Norwegian.

When it comes to history the speakers are not around any more, and scholars may therefore propose very remarkable ideas about what languages were spoken in earlier periods, more or less with impunity. Some have maintained that since the spoken language in Rome changed as early as in antiquity, so that features were introduced that are also found later on in the Romance languages Italian, Spanish, French, and so on, the Romans in reality did not speak Latin but a Romance language as early as around AD 150. But if we know anything for sure about the people in the Roman Empire at that time it is that they knew when they spoke Latin, the very language of the empire. Further, people did believe that they spoke that language as long as the empire existed, and long after that.

But for how long can a language exist? We know that all languages change constantly, and after a number of centuries they have changed so much that documents written in the old language are no longer understandable. Is it still the same language, or another one?

The answer is that this depends on the view of the speakers themselves. Latin has disappeared, as people in Italy, France, and Spain do not consider themselves to speak Latin. But Arabic is still around, ever since the seventh century AD, and the people in a vast area, from Morocco to Syria, agree that they speak Arabic, although the spoken language forms in different parts of the area are very dissimilar, and neither do they closely resemble the spoken language of the seventh century. The views of people on this matter obviously have something to do with what the language sounds like and who understands it, but those are by no means the only relevant facts, and perhaps not even the most important ones.

LATIN AND FRENCH

Around AD 800 something significant happened in European history; it also had consequences for the history of languages. Charlemagne formed a large empire, becoming the overlord of large parts of modern France, Germany, and neighbouring countries. He introduced a reform of the system of education so that many more people, mainly clergymen, learned to read and write correctly. The language they learned was of course Latin, and their norm was classical Latin, the written language used in Rome in the centuries around AD 1. This meant a considerable change from the written language of the preceding centuries, which had been heavily influenced by spoken language.

One of the consequences of this was that the few people who could read and write came to regard spoken language as something quite different from written language. The relation between spoken and written forms, which may have been taken more for granted before the reform, became problematic when the written language was supposed to adhere to an old and strange model. As a consequence they soon felt a need to write down what was actually said, rather than something vaguely similar in correct, classical Latin.

The first time we know that this happened is in a relation of contemporary events that was written in the 840s. It is of course written in Latin, as almost everything was at that time. The author, by the name of Nithard, tells about an important meeting in 842 between Louis the German and Charles the Bald, two of the sons of Louis the Pious. These two men had decided to join their forces and go to war against their brother, Lothar, the third son of Louis, in order to share the Carolingian Empire among the two of them. They met in Strasbourg, each with his army. Charles the Bald brought his troops from France and Louis the German came with his men from Germany. They swore solemn oaths in front of the armies. Louis the German had to swear the oath in the language of France in order for Charles's army to understand it, and Charles, in reciprocation, swore in German. This was something quite unusual, and that is probably why the oaths were written down exactly in the way they were spoken. In that way, a few lines rendering the spoken language in France in the ninth century have been preserved. Some phrases of the oath spoken by Louis:

D'ist di in avant, in quant Deus savir et podir me dunat, si salvarai eo cist meon fradre Karlo

Learned scholars have thought much about this text. It would have been something like this in tolerably classical Latin:

De isto die inantea, in quantum mihi Deus scire et posse donaverit, sic salvabo istum meum fratrem Karolum

In English, this would mean:

From this day and onwards, in so far as God gives me knowledge and capacity, I will support this brother of mine Charles.

It is easy to see that the text of the oath does not look like Latin. It is true that the vocabulary is largely the same. But Latin has, among other things, a complicated system of endings attached to nouns and adjectives. This system has changed drastically: *ist-o di-e*, with endings attached to both words, corresponds to *ist di*, without any endings. The inflection of verbs is also quite different. The form *salvarai*, "I will support," is particularly remarkable. It corresponds to the Latin verb *salvabo*. The form of the oath can be traced back to two Latin verbs in sequence, *salvare habeo*. Thus, while the language form in the oath of Louis has many words in common with classical Latin, the rules for inflection, and much else besides, are different. It seems obvious that written Latin at this time was quite different from the spoken language.

It is often said that the Strasbourg oath is the first example of a new language, Old French. There is something to this, of course. From a linguistic point of view, the text looks more like French than Latin, which shows that many features of modern French existed in the spoken language as early as in the ninth century. By the way, it is interesting that the first quoted speaker of French was Louis the German. It is no accident that the Carolingian Empire is often seen as a forerunner to the European Union.

On the other hand, it would be a mistake to assume that Louis and Charles and their armies thought of Latin and the spoken language as two wholly separate entities. The languages that were clearly different were, on the one hand the language used in Germany, *theotisca lingua,* as it is called in Latin, and on the other hand the language spoken in France, which was normally written as Latin when it was written. On this occasion it was important to know exactly what was said, in the way illiterate people understood it, and that is why it was written down in that manner. This does not mean that Nithard or anyone else thought that there existed another language than Latin in France. And if they had thought that, they obviously would not have considered themselves to speak Old French.

Considerably later, in the early decades of the eleventh century, there appeared in France texts written in a language that was not Latin. Slightly later still there is proof that the ones writing in this language also had a name for it. It was sometimes called *Roman,* and sometimes *François.* At this time, then, it is proper to say that French first appears.

One may ask why people started writing in a new language instead of sticking to Latin. One answer is of course that Latin and the spoken language had at this time diverged very much. But there was a more important reason. At this time, a new group of prospective readers emerged.

The long period from the fall of the Roman Empire in the fifth century through to the eleventh century is a rather bleak time in Europe in terms of education and culture as well as of economic development. The towns of the Romans were dilapidated and emptied, the roads were not used, and almost all people lived as poor farmers in the countryside. When written language was used at all it was handled by the few educated people, who were found within the Church and received their education within her schools. The language of the Church remained Latin.

But a long period of rise had its start in the later part of the eleventh century. The economy improved, and so did communications. It became more frequent that those who could afford it received an education even if they were not interested in a career within the Church. There appeared a class of educated noblemen who lived in their castles or manors, with money and time at their disposal. They might like to read, but they had no taste for theology or saints' lives. This environment is the birthplace of medieval love songs, heroic tales, and, in due time, epic romances. These were the kinds of texts written in French.

However, contracts, laws, and similar official documents are not to be found in French to begin with. It is of course very important that the people involved understand such documents, and so one might have expected the use of French, the written language close to the spoken one. But Latin stayed in use for such purposes for a long time. Thus, the new written language was not introduced because it was useful in business or in court.

Latin was evidently considered to work well enough in such contexts.

Coming back to the question of when French first appeared, one can observe that the name of the language first appears as a designation for the written language. Once there are texts written in French, the name French, *François*, also appears. Before that, people spoke something that was not very similar to Latin for several hundred years. But the language does not receive a name of its own until a separate written language exists.

Did Latin cease to exist at the same time? Definitely not. In the first place, people continued writing and reading Latin for hundreds of years, both in France and in other countries. Secondly, *François* was the name only for the language of northern France, but the formerly Latin-speaking area was much larger. It is time to have a look at the other countries.

OC, OIL, AND SI

At the time when French became a written language in northern France, another form of writing appeared in the area which is now southern France. The language of this region is called Occitan, and the main dialect, on which the written language is based, is Provençal. In practice, the two names are often used interchangeably. It was used in writing for a few hundred years in the Middle Ages, and again in a period of revival in the nineteenth century. At present the written form is found only to a very modest extent. As a spoken language Occitan is now retreating in favour of French, the official language of the state.

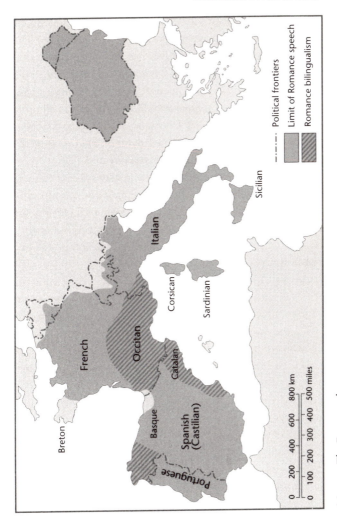

MAP 4. The Romance languages

The medieval texts are chiefly troubadour poems, love songs in a highly artistic language with complex verse technique. The troubadours and their audiences were found in the many courts around queens, dukes, counts, and other important people in the rich region of Provence. This poetry in fact represented a new, more sophisticated and refined way of life, and it was admired and imitated all over Europe. Everyone wanted to be a troubadour, yearning for the unattainable lady of his heart—or be the object of a troubadour's yearning, as the case may be.

In this way two Romance written languages appeared almost at the same time, French in northern France and Provençal in southern France. They developed and stabilized during the twelfth and the thirteenth centuries. In the thirteenth century a third written Romance language made its appearance, the one that is nowadays called Italian.

However, a quite different name was used to begin with. The first people to write anything other than Latin in the Italian region were found in Sicily in the beginning of the twelfth century, at the famous court of Frederick II in Palermo. There, poets who are now all pretty much forgotten wrote troubadour poems in the Provençal style, but in the language of the island. Dante, who lived a couple of generations later, says that "all poetry written by Italians is called Sicilian" and that the language in which it is written is called *sicilianum vulgare*. He thinks that will be the case in the future too. And possibly Italian would still have been called Sicilian, had not Dante himself come along.

Dante Alighieri, 1265–1321, is the famous poet chiefly known for *La divina commedia*, *The Divine Comedy*. He also was extremely interested in language problems. He wrote his poems in the language we call Italian, but he also produced several books in Latin. One of them deals with languages and is called *De vulgari eloquentia*, which means approximately "How to write in the popular language."

In that book he first surveys the language situation of Europe, as he sees it, but the aim of the book is to investigate which is the best (written) language for use in Italy. The time was ripe for establishing the third Romance written language, and Dante knew that he was the man to do it. His treatise tells us how one can choose a written language, and it is composed by the very person who made the choice.

First, Dante briefly surveys the languages of the world, leaning heavily on what is said about the Creation in the Bible. It may be noted that Dante is somewhat bothered by the fact that (in his reading of the text) the first human to speak is Eve when answering the serpent, and not Adam. But he brushes this aside, laying down as a matter of course that it would be improper for such an achievement to have its origin in woman and not in man, and so Adam must still have received speech first, straight from the Creator.

After the unfortunate construction of the tower of Babel the language was confounded according to the Bible, and Dante says that Europe had three languages to begin with. He calls them *idyomata*, using the Greek word we have in the form "idiom." The first language is Greek, the second one a language that later developed into various languages in the north and east, such as German, English, Slavic languages, and Hungarian. That there are certain important differences between those languages was clearly not known to Dante. The third "idiom" is the one spoken in western Europe, and about that he had considerable knowledge.

That language, he says, really is one and the same, even though it now seems to be tripartite. That it is basically one language is clear from the fact that almost all words are common. On the other hand there are differences between the three groups, and one is how "yes" is expressed: the Spaniards say *oc*, the Franks, *oïl*, and the Italians, *sì*.

This is the very first description of three different forms of Romance speech. However, for us it is easy to read into the text a few things that are not actually stated there. In the first place, it is clear from the context that what we call Spanish actually does not figure at all. The people Dante calls "Spaniards" (*Yspani*) are according to himself all people in southern Europe living west of Genoa, in north-west Italy. As a matter of fact he means the Occitan language, and he thinks that it is spoken all over the Pyrenean peninsula, which has, of course, never been the case. But in Provençal "yes" is *oc*, true enough; in fact that is why the language is called *Oc*citan.

As for the Franks, Dante means French, which was a well-established literary language. Actually his partition is not really made to reflect different ways of speaking, though it may seem so at first. He divides the area according to the new written languages. French, which is well established, gets its due share, and Provençal, equally prestigious, receives much more than that. The third part Dante reserves for the written language which he uses himself and which is just about to be generally accepted in Italy.

Dante calls each of the three forms *vulgare*, which means approximately "popular language" or perhaps "dialect," and does not use *ydioma*, "language."

The main problem in Dante's treatise is what the written language in Italy should look like. As a preliminary, he first surveys the spoken language of different parts of Italy. To my knowledge it is the first investigation of dialects ever made, and it is both competent and entertaining. For a start he denounces the Roman way of speaking, "the most shameful of all Italian dialects." The only accent that may be even worse is Sardic, as it is far too close to Latin. Dante thinks that the Sards of Sardinia imitate Latin "like apes." The spoken forms that are treated less rudely are those that had already been used in writing, such as Sicilian, Tuscan (Dante's own dialect), and the language of Bologna.

The final conclusion, however, is that no dialect can be used without modification. A proper and fitting written language, a *vulgare illustre*, has to contain the features common to most of the dialects but no peculiarities from anyone.

This may not sound very remarkable to us. People have thought in similar ways later on in several parts of the world when new written languages have been created. But Dante was first. Also, he is quite different from later language planners, who have typically been educators in states with a strong language. Dante is an artist and an intellectual. He is a refugee from one small state in Italy, and has spent his life wandering from one small state to another. No one before him has proposed that these small states, and many similar ones, are bonded through a common language.

But this is precisely his point. Dante is not only a linguist and an artist; he is just as much a politician and an ideologist. He dreamt of another dispensation in Italy, an emperor governing the entire land, with a brilliant court around him. The language of this court would be exactly the language form proposed by Dante. As a matter of fact, in his view a real *vulgare illustre* has to be connected with a court (or courts). That was true for Provençal and even more for French, and if the new language was to rise to the level of those, Italy should have a really important ruler, an emperor with his court.

This way of thinking tells much about Dante himself and his position. It also tells some important things about the function and position of the new Romance languages, and about why they appeared at all.

What happened was not at all that people in general started talking about their languages as French, Provençal, or Italian instead of calling it Latin. We mostly know very little about what people in general called the language they spoke during the Middle Ages. Our written sources usually do not deal with such matters. They mention written languages such as Latin, Greek, and Hebrew, and later on French and other modern languages, when they become written languages. But if ordinary people had been asked what they spoke the chances are that the answers would include names like the ones Dante provides for various Italian dialects: Apulian, Bolognese, Sicilian, and so on.

The new written languages are created by linguistically sophisticated people, well versed in Latin, from various spoken dialects. This first happened in northern France and in Provence, then in Italy and Spain, still later in Portugal, and last in Romania.

The Romance area did not split into different languages because of any inevitable dialectal changes or any particularly great differences in the spoken language. Instead, new written forms for artistic expression were created by authors and other well-educated people who usually were found in the courts, very close to the political power.

Thus the new languages were primarily vehicles for literature, but they were also in some measure expressions of political power. It did mean something that French people in the ascending French kingdom were able to express themselves in writing in their own language, not only in Latin, a truly international language with a special connection to the Church that held almost a monopoly on learning and had much political strength. The new languages could also provide some breathing-space for those who did not fully appreciate the dominance of the Church.

Dante wished to create a new language for Italy, and the reason was precisely that he wanted a new, politically coherent country. He succeeded, in a way. Not perhaps because of his ideas, but for the reason that he produced marvellous works of art in the new language. *The Divine Comedy* became a linguistic model, and made Italian one of the European languages. The very fact that Italy had a common written language and a common literary heritage meant very much during the following centuries; it provided strong support for the idea that Italy ought to become a political entity. As is well known, the state of Italy came into being in the mid-nineteenth century, more than 500 years after Dante's time.

Did Dante Write in Italian?

Even though Dante was the first great Italian writer, it may be questioned whether he wrote in Italian. This is less strange than it seems to be. Dante very consciously designed a new language norm and used it in his poetical works. What he did not do was to assign a name to the new language.

When Dante writes in Latin he uses the term *vulgare* for the new languages. He talks about three different ones, and the one used in Italy he calls *Latium vulgare*, "the Latin popular language." It is true that he speaks about Italians, *Ytali*, but he does not use that word in connection with the name of the language. As for Latin, the learned language in which he himself wrote, he also employs a fairly remarkable name. He consistently calls it *Grammatica*, "Grammar." And when Dante writes in Italian, he uses another astonishing term; he sometimes mentions the language he is writing in, and calls it *Latino*, "Latin."

To us this is extremely confusing, and it shows that Dante did not think of Latin as one language and Italian as a completely different one, which is the common view nowadays. In his mind there really existed only one language, which manifested itself either as written Latin or as one of the written popular languages. Dante did not regard Latin as the origin of the popular languages, but rather he apprehended it as a common way of writing, unaffected by dialectal differences. In that respect, his approach was completely ahistorical.

But later generations had other ideas. The language of Dante became a model for many authors, and soon after his death a name for this new written language became current. In the language, the term was *italiano*, "Italian," or *lingua italiana*, "the Italian language." So Dante and his predecessors created a new written language, but it did not receive a name of its own until later.

The situation was similar in northern France and in Provence. The new French written language developed before a name for it was generally recognized. For quite some time it was called either *roman* or *françois*, until the latter name finally prevailed. In Provence, there never was any final agreement on the name of the language. Even today, one finds the competing designations *provençal* or *occitan* or *langue d'oc*.

This concern about the exact names of languages may seem finicky. But I maintained earlier that what is crucial for the existence of a language is whether people think it exists. If that is correct, then the language name is really very important. For one cannot easily speak about something which cannot be named, and those who cannot talk about a language probably do not regard it as anything of real importance.

That is why I think that Italian did not exist as a language in its own right until the name *italiano* was in general use. This was in the mid-fourteenth century or a little before that, about a generation after Dante. And who were those who spoke about Italian? Those people who read and wrote the new written language, a small minority of well-educated people in the rich merchant cities of Italy. Ordinary people probably did not hear about the language until quite some time later. If they had occasion to talk about the matter they would probably consider themselves to speak the local idiom, such as *mantovano*, "the Mantua dialect," while the written language was Latin, as it had always been.

This changed, and people in general in Italy came to think that they actually spoke Italian, as is the universal opinion today. When this happened really is not known; probably it was a gradual and fairly slow process. One may guess that as written Italian became more known and more used, people became more inclined to think that they actually spoke Italian, the language used in writing.

So the order of events was that a written language was created first; then it acquired a name, Italian; and at last, the same name was adopted for the spoken language. Though the spoken language is always basic, and any kind of writing is an imitation of speech, it was the new written form that made people think of their way of speaking as a language, separate from other languages.

This is true not only for Italy, and not only for the Romance languages. Writing means a lot to our perception of languages. Briefly, if there is an independent manner of writing, there is a language, otherwise not. People have tended to think so in the past, and most people think so today.

DID DANTE WRITE IN LATIN?

> Nel mezzo del cammin di nostra vita
> mi ritrovai per una selva oscura . . .

A translation:

> Midway in the journey of our life
> I found myself in a dark wood . . .

This is the beginning of the *Divine Comedy*. It is not entirely easy to understand that Dante considered himself to be writing in something that could be called *latino*, "Latin," for this language is really very far removed from ordinary written Latin, and on the whole quite close to modern Italian. An attempt to translate the lines above into pedestrian classical Latin might yield something like this:

> In medio cursu vitae nostrae
> eram in silva obscura . . .

A Roman poet would have written more elegantly, but he would not have been closer to Dante's text. The languages are different in several ways. For example, Latin has no indefinite article like English "a" or "an," but Italian has; the form is *uno* or *una*. Thus, "a dark forest" is *silva obscura* in Latin but *una selva oscura* in Dante's text. Further, possession in Latin is expressed by an ending, analogous to the *'s* in English, but Italian must use the preposition *di*, analogous to English *of*: compare Latin *vitae nostrae* "our life's" (*-e* represents the Latin ending) and Dante's *di nostra vita* "of our life." There are many differences of that kind, and in addition much dissimilarity in the vocabulary. For example, *mezzo* and *medio* represent the same word, historically speaking, but the pronunciation has changed a great deal. The words *cammin* and *ritrovai* used by Dante do not exist at all in Latin, and are derived from Celtic and from Greek, respectively. Taken together, those changes make it impossible for a person who knows only Italian to understand Latin right away, as well as the other way around.

Evidently, there were linguistic reasons for the creation of the Romance written languages. The ancient Latin written form had become so different from the spoken languages that learning to read and write was almost like learning an entirely foreign language. But this reform was not brought about spontaneously or gradually by people who felt that the old written language was just too hard to handle. The new written forms were invented by well-educated and determined people who were closely associated with centres of political power. The effects of their reforms were fundamental, especially in the long run. It was not just a matter of writing in another way; the writing and the new literature changed people's perceptions about the language itself. And perceptions about one's language have a lot to do with perceptions about one's identity. Where people had earlier seen themselves just as Mantuans or Florentines, many began to think of themselves also as Italians. That in turn had important consequences for history.

Chapter 7

From Germanic to Modern English

HOW ENGLISH CAME TO BRITAIN

The English language emerged as a separate, identifiable unit much earlier than the Romance languages discussed in the previous chapter. One reason for this is the situation in England after the fall of the Roman Empire, so we have to start with what happened in that period.

The Romans conquered Britain in the first century AD and held it for 300 years. Yet, as was noted above, Latin did not become the spoken language, as it did in present-day France, Spain, and Portugal. The reasons can only be guessed. People in Britain retained their language, which belonged to the Celtic group of Indo-European languages. That language is nowadays sometimes called British, and sometimes Brythonic; the modern language Welsh is a descendant of it, and so was the Cornish language (in Cornwall) that ceased to be spoken as a native language around 1800.

Around the year 400, the Roman troops in Britain were summoned to the mainland because of the crisis there, and Roman governors and tax collectors are not heard of any more. The British were left to fend for themselves. This was no easy task in the turbulent fifth century. Sure enough, the island was soon invaded from two directions. In the north, which had never been held by the Romans, the Irish, who spoke a quite different Celtic language, occupied the western coastland and later much more. The descendant of the Irish language there is now usually called Scots Gaelic. In the north there were also Picts, a little-known people who had a language of their own.

But the most dramatic invasion came from the east. Germanic groups from the southern and eastern coast of the North Sea looked for opportunities in different parts of the disintegrating empire. They found very little resistance in the island. Actually, the first Germans are said to have come in three ships in the year 449, invited by the Britons to help them against the Irish invaders from the north and west.

More Germans followed; most of them belonged to two groups named Angles and Saxons. They rapidly expanded over most of the island, forming a large number of small independent kingdoms. After a century and a half, around the year 600, they dominated most of England. The Britons were pushed back to Wales and Cornwall, and the Scots from Ireland held Scotland.

What is very remarkable is that the language shifted over the whole conquered area. The Germans were able to impose their language in less than 300 years where the Romans could not impose theirs. How come? Probably because they came in larger numbers and wanted to farm the land themselves. Possibly they also systematically chased away or killed the Britons, although that is not easy to know. What is obvious is that the new states kept no traditions from Romans or Britons: they were just Germanic kingdoms.

The situation in the island is summed up at the beginning of the *Peterborough Chronicle* (which is one version of the *Anglo-Saxon Chronicle*), a text probably written in the tenth century:

Brittene igland is ehta hund mila lang & twa hund brad, & her sind on þis iglande fif gebeode: Englisc & Brittisc . . . & Scyttisc & Pyhtisc & Boc Leden.

A word-for-word translation into modern English:

Britain's island is eight hundred miles long and two hundred broad, and there are on this island five languages: English and British . . . and Scottish and Pictish and Book Latin.

Although the old text may not be easy to decipher without the translation, it can be rendered word for word in modern English, and most of the words are obviously related, sometimes identical. It is clearly an old form of English, and the language is called "Englisc" by the author.

Thus, English had a name, and was used as a written language, hundreds of years before French and Italian. Why? To answer that question, it is necessary to have a closer look at the background of the Germans who came to England, and also at the situation that confronted them when they came.

MAP 5. The languages of Britain in Bede's time

GERMANS, ANGLES, SAXONS

When the Romans built up their empire in southern and western Europe, they were brought into contact and conflict with the Germans, who lived in the east and north. Julius Caesar, who led the conquest of Gaul around 50 BC, extended Roman domination to all lands west of the Rhine, and that river henceforth marked the border against the Germans. The linguistic frontier between Romance and Germanic languages still largely follows the river.

The Germans were not held together by any common bond, but were grouped into a large number of small, independent states. We know about their ways of life and about the different states from a number of Latin and Greek sources. The most important one is a small book about the Germans by the Roman historian Tacitus, written in AD 98. The author is best known in England for his biography of Agricola, his father-in-law, who spent several years as a general in Britain.

The Angles are mentioned in passing by Tacitus, together with a number of now forgotten neighbours. He talks about "Reudigni . . . et Aviones et Anglii et Varini et Eudoses et Suardones et Nuitones" as peoples who lived in present-day Schleswig and Mecklenburg, by the coast of the North Sea and the south-western Baltic. There is nothing remarkable about the individual groups, he says, but they have in common a cult of Nerthus, Mother Earth.

If Tacitus is right, and there is no real reason for doubt, the Angles at this time were a quite insignificant band, living in a fairly small area beside six other similar groups. The number of

Angles must have been very modest, hardly more than a few thousand people.

The Saxons are not even mentioned by Tacitus, but appear in other sources about a century later. Towards the fourth century, they gained some notoriety as raiders along the coast of Roman Gaul, from the Rhine as far down as the Loire.

So, the Angles and Saxons were small Germanic groups originally living along the North Sea coast beside their Germanic neighbours. What about their language, or languages?

Tacitus and other Roman authors say little about the language of the Germans. Still, there is good evidence to prove that the Germans at this time all spoke in a fairly similar way, although of course there were dialectal differences over the vast area. Germans at this time occupied the better part of present-day Germany, the Netherlands, and southern Scandinavia. Nowadays, the hypothetical common language is often called Germanic or Proto-Germanic.

Did that language have a name of its own? Probably not. No contemporary sources mention a Germanic language. The words *Germania*, "Germany," and *Germani*, "Germans," are found in Latin texts, but it is not known whether the Germans themselves used these words. The origin of the word is not known. It is very much in doubt whether the peoples who spoke Germanic saw themselves as a coherent group in any context whatsoever. If they did not, they had no need for a common name.

THE LANGUAGE OF THE ANGLES AND SAXONS

The Saxons invaded the south of England, and formed three kingdoms along the coast of the Channel: Essex, Sussex, and Wessex. The Angles dominated in the area north of the Thames, with the kingdoms East Anglia, Middle Anglia, Mercia, and Northumbria; the latter stretched all the way north to the Firth of Forth.

Did they come with separate Anglian and Saxon languages, or with an Anglo-Saxon language? Probably neither. There can hardly be any question of talking about two separate languages, for sources indicate that there were no great differences between the speech in the south and in the north, and that people could readily understand each other all over the area. On the other hand, Angles and Saxons were in no way united before their arrival in England. And there were other invaders too. Kent and the Isle of Wight were taken by the Jutes (presumably from Jutland, although that has been questioned), and modern scholars tend to believe that there were many Frisians among the newcomers.

So the Germanic language imported to England was not the particular property of any one ethnic group. It was the language spoken along a considerable stretch of the North Sea coast, probably with appreciable dialectal variations. It was part of a larger continuous sweep of dialects that extended farther south, and east, and north along the peninsula of Jutland.

Thus, where the immigrants came from they were surrounded by people who spoke more or less like themselves, and language was hardly an important criterion for deciding to which group one belonged. But this was different in the island where they arrived.

The people who were already there spoke British, or Scottish, or Pictish, three languages that were quite different from each other, and did not resemble Germanic languages at all. The newcomers formed a new language group, with another culture and other political aspirations as well. The internal dialectal differences within the group meant little compared to the large similarities. The invaders were no doubt regarded as one group by the speakers of other languages. No doubt they also saw themselves as a body in many contexts, in contrast to the Britons. On the other hand, they were not politically united but lived in a number of small, independent kingdoms.

One has to ask, then, when the English language appeared, in the sense that people in Britain started thinking about the Germanic language as an entity of its own. It has been seen above that the Romance languages acquired their own identities when written forms were created, and that names for the languages appeared at the same time or a little later. In Britain, one can note the same sequence of events.

However, the situation is somewhat more complex, as two different scripts are involved. We have to discuss runes first, and then the more important Latin script.

RUNES IN BRITAIN

Even though the Germanic peoples may not have regarded themselves as one group, they did use a system of writing adapted for their language, the runes.

It is believed nowadays that the script was invented around the first century AD. It is an alphabetic script, so the general idea must reasonably have been picked up from the Latin alphabet used by the Romans. Still, the runic script is a quite free adaptation. Letters consist mostly of straight lines; the system was clearly adapted for carving in wood. Some letters resemble the Latin ones, like ᛒ for B and ᛏ for T, but many have been much altered or are just different, like ᚠ for F and ᛗ for D. Some letters have no correspondents in Latin, and denote sounds found in Germanic languages, notably ᚦ for a dental fricative, the first sound in *thing*, and ᛈ for a velar glide, the first sound in *we*.

The earliest runic inscriptions are from around AD 200, and the runes had a long history, especially in Scandinavia, where they remained in use for a thousand years and more.

Among the early Germanic invaders in Britain, there were some who knew the runic script. The earliest testimony of the new language in the island is an inscription on a bone from a deer, found in an urn dating from the fourth or fifth century. It runs ᚱᚨᛁᚺᚨᚾ, which should probably be transliterated *raihan*. There is no clue to the meaning, unfortunately, although the sequence of letters looks as if it might represent some unknown Germanic word.

In the first two hundred years, up to around 650, runic script is found mainly in the south-east and south, in East Anglia and in Kent. The number and the shapes of letters in Britain differ somewhat from the common practice on the Continent, mainly as a result of adaptations of the script to the spoken language. Thus, there is a distinctive Anglo-Saxon runic alphabet.

In the south and south-west the use of runes seems to have faded as early as around 650. This is not really surprising, for inscriptions could be made in Latin script instead, as will be discussed presently.

In the midlands and the north, above all in Northumbria, the runes were employed regularly from the seventh century through to the eleventh in Christian contexts. A natural way to interpret this is that in this area, the Church chose to appropriate the old runic script for its own purposes. There must have been a good reason. Most probably, some people could read runic inscriptions in their own language, but not Latin letters. It is also possible that the Church took an interest because this was a way to eliminate the association between runes and magical practices connected to the old religion.

So, was the Anglo-Saxon runic script the original way to write English? The answer cannot be an unqualified yes. Undeniably, the runic script was used for the Germanic language in Britain before the Roman one. But was it the English language? When the runes were first used, people may not yet have thought of the Germanic language in Britain as one unit, separated from those on the Continent. Before they went out of use, this notion was certainly firmly established. But it does not seem that the use of runes had any significant impact in that process. They cannot have been used very much, and are almost completely unattested in a large part of south-western England. On the whole, they remained a marginal phenomenon. Written English arose in another way.

THE ROMAN SCRIPT AND ENGLISH

After the invasions around 450, the Latin language virtually disappeared from the part of Britain inhabited by the Germans. Among the Irish and the Britons, who were Christians, knowledge of the language was maintained within the Church, but in the heathen Germanic kingdoms Latin had no place whatsoever. This also meant, of course, that the Roman script was not in use. For more than a century, there was only the runic script.

When the first Christian missionaries arrived from Rome, they brought with them not only the faith and the Latin language, but also the Latin alphabet, parchment, and pen. This new technology made it relatively easy to produce long written texts, something that had been impossible in practice as long as only runes were available. Very soon, people availed themselves of the opportunity to use the new script for the vernacular language.

In 597, Pope Gregory sent the Roman prelate Augustine as a missionary to Britain, with a party of followers. They were well received by the king of Kent, Ethelbert, who already knew about the Christian faith. He had married Bertha, a Frankish princess of the Merovingian dynasty, who was a Christian and had brought with her from Paris a personal chaplain. Ethelbert himself converted to the Christian faith, and Augustine became the first archbishop of Canterbury, which was at that time the main town in Kent.

Augustine and his followers were of course literate in Latin, which was the written language of Rome and of the Church, and they brought books with them. A correspondence between

Augustine and Pope Gregory is preserved; there is even a letter from the pope to King Ethelbert. Canterbury became a bridgehead for knowledge of Latin.

From these modest beginnings, the Latin language was to spread all over Britain together with the Christian faith, so that within a century it was firmly established across the island. However, the most remarkable linguistic result of the mission was that the Latin way of writing was almost immediately appropriated for the vernacular language of Kent.

The first English text written in the Latin alphabet is the law of Ethelbert, perhaps produced as early as 603, only a few years after the arrival of the missionaries, and at any rate not later than 616, when Ethelbert died. The text has been preserved in a manuscript from the twelfth century, unfortunately in a modernized form. It is fairly short and consists mainly of a list of fines for various offences. An example:

> Gif man frigne man gebindep, XX scill' gebete.
>
> "If a man binds a free man, he should pay 20 shilling."

There are several questions one may ask about this. From where did the king get the idea to create a written law? Who benefited from it? Why was it written in the vernacular, and not in Latin? How was the new written language created? Although we know little about the king and his kingdom, some answers may be suggested.

The idea of a written law was not new. Roman laws were in writing, of course, and this one was not the first Germanic law to be written down. The several Germanic groups had partly similar customary laws that had no doubt been transmitted orally for a long time. Some of the peoples who had entered the Roman Empire felt a need for codification in Latin, the written language of their new homelands. The most famous of those written Germanic laws was that of the Salian Franks, which exists in a Latin version from around 500. Bertha, the Frankish princess who was Ethelbert's wife, must have known about that law.

The promulgation of a law is a political act, and is normally done for some specific purpose. In this case, it is not difficult to see who stood to gain from the new situation. The bulk of the law seems to list well-established regulations, but the first paragraph is quite different. It stipulates exorbitant fines for offences against the Church, the bishop, and other ecclesiastics. In a society where the Christian Church had existed for only a few years, this must have been sensational. Clearly, one object of the law was to further the interests of the Church and the new religion.

At the same time, the king himself derived some profit. He proclaimed a law in his own name together with this council, *witan*. In the Germanic states, law was originally seen as a tradition of the people rather than as decrees from the rulers. The Salic law, for example was based on records of practices collected by four chosen men from local leaders. Ethelbert was one of the first Germanic kings to put his name on a written law. This obviously meant something for his prestige and for the relations between him and his *witan*.

The law was not written in Latin, the language of the Church. One may guess the reason: it would have been pointless, as the readership would have been almost non-existent. To do it in English was also problematic from the point of view of communication, for no one was a trained reader of English before the existence of any texts in the language. Possibly an acquaintance with the runes alleviated the learning process for some Kentish leaders, but some education within the Church would have been necessary anyhow. Certainly only a small number of specialists were able to read the law to begin with. Still, it was written, and that was a pioneering move that would have momentous consequences, for it marked the beginning of English as a literary language.

As for the new way of writing, it was probably not exceedingly difficult to devise. In most cases, Latin letters could be used to represent English sounds. We do not know who produced the text, but it might have been a joint effort involving literate missionaries and legally minded Kentish people. As the text is not preserved in its original state we are also ignorant about the exact spelling conventions adopted at this first stage. Old English texts in general mainly employ the same Latin letters still used to write English. The main difference is that a few letters were borrowed from the runic script to represent sounds not found in Latin. Two have been mentioned above, namely Þ for voiceless *th*, as in *thing*, and Ƿ for *w*; in addition, there was ð for voiced *th*, as in *them*.

So, the text was the first document written in Latin letters in the Germanic language of Britain, and the king has a good claim to the position of the father of written English. He may not have held a pen himself, or even been able to read, but he must have given the appropriate orders, and thus the text is king Ethelbert's law. But behind the scene, the important players may have been two immigrants, Archbishop Augustine and Queen Bertha.

THE FIRST CENTURIES OF ENGLISH LITERATURE

The new way of writing English was hardly used frequently to begin with. During the seventh century two more legal texts were produced in Kent, and at the end of the century King Ine of Wessex produced a law of his own. After that, no laws may have been written down for almost 200 years. There are just a few other administrative documents.

Another kind of literature flourished, however, namely poetry. We know that at least one person composed poetry in English during the seventh century, and several important poets (mainly anonymous) followed his example in subsequent centuries. Most of the poems are preserved in a few manuscripts written around AD 1000, and cannot be dated very precisely, so it is hard to say how early the best pieces are. Nor can we know whether the authors wrote them down or they were transmitted orally until someone committed them to writing.

The poets used a metre that was never used in Latin, but obviously belonged to a long oral tradition of Germanic poetry. Most of their works treated Christian topics, but a few well-known ones take up themes from Germanic lore. The most famous poem by far is about a Geat, which means a person from Götaland in Sweden (at least according to the opinion of this writer, who is fond of that province). The Geat's name is revealed only after more than 300 lines of verse, when the hero arrives with his men to the hall of the king of Danes to offer his services:

> We synt Higelaces
> beodgeneatas; Beowulf is min nama.

> Wille ic asecgan sunu Healfdenes,
> mærum peodne, min ærende.
>
> "We are Hygelac's
> table-companions; Beowulf is my name.
> I wish to say to the son of Halfdane,
> the famous ruler, my errand."

This dignified self-presentation provides an example of early English poetry. Each verse consists of two halves, with a pause in between, and with two stressed syllables in each half, as in *mæ´rum þe´odne, mi´n æ´rende.* Further, one syllable in each half of the verse has to start with the same consonant; they alliterate with each other. In the verse just quoted, the alliteration is between m*ærum* and m*in*.

The hero volunteers to fight the monster Grendel that is haunting the Danes. The setting, the story, and the mood of the poem are as alien to the Latin culture of the Christian missionaries as the meter (even though the author of *Beowulf* is in fact a Christian himself). The new written language was used also to propagate works of art that did not derive their inspiration from the religion through which the writing system was introduced.

It seems that English literature during the first few centuries consisted only of legal texts and poetry. Both kinds of text are remarkably independent of Latin models. It is true that there are several poems of Christian inspiration, but they owe little or nothing to Latin examples when it comes to style and meter. Still, the writers must have had their literary training in the schools of the Church, as there were no others. Obviously, they were in no way overwhelmed by foreign learning.

This may say something about the circles in which those people moved. They must have been close to the leading group, who were in charge of laws and who could find the time necessary to memorize and transmit the important traditional stories. At the same time, they had close connections with the new Church. All this points to environments around the ruling kings in the various Germanic kingdoms: Kent, Wessex, Mercia, and so on. The political resources were found there, and also the Christian learning, for the policy of the Roman mission was to start at the top in society, establishing close relations with the rulers for mutual benefit. The monasteries, centres of education, were in several cases governed by abbesses from royal families.

In those days there was no central authority among the Germanic kingdoms of Britain, but probably some sense of cultural unity, and some co-operation in wars against the Britons. This had certain consequences for the literary products. The few authors probably often knew of each other. Still there were no attempts at creating a common standard for the written language. On the contrary, each writer employed his own local dialect, so there are texts in Kentish, in West Saxon, in Northumbrian, and so on.

This is quite similar to the situation in Greece before the Macedonian conquest, and to some extent also to that of Italy before Dante. Where there is no political unity, the idea of a common standard for a written language is not very close at hand. Even though the writers of Britain probably all knew the strictly standardized written Latin language, they did not try to create anything similar. Possibly they were on the way towards different local standards, so that there would have been a

Northumbrian written dialect, a Kentish written dialect, and so on, just as Greece at one time had Doric, Ionic, and Aeolic. However, history moved in another direction.

BEDE, LATIN, AND ENGLISH

Within less than a century from the arrival of Augustine in 597, all the Anglo-Saxon kingdoms were at least nominally Christian. The detailed story about this is told by Bede in his remarkable *History of the Church of the English People,* finished soon after 730. Bede was a monk and a priest in the monasteries of Monkwearmouth and Jarrow, in present-day Newcastle-upon-Tyne.

The work is written in Latin, and very good Latin at that. Bede was a prolific writer. The ecclesiastical history is his best-known work, but he also produced voluminous commentaries to most books of the Bible, and much else besides. He was an exceptional man, but the fact that he could accomplish all this in a monastery in Northumbria in the early eighth century is in itself good evidence that Anglo-Saxon Britain had become a place where the Latin language was important.

This does not necessarily mean that there were large numbers of people who were able to speak, read, and write in Latin. Most probably only a fairly small number of persons possessed those skills, and most of them were ecclesiastics. As all the native languages of Britain were completely different from Latin, one had to learn that language in schools of some kind, and such schools were almost certainly found only within the Church.

The Christian religion and the Latin language were imported together, and depended on each other. Preaching to the laymen must have been in the spoken language, but the Bible, the liturgy, the hymns, the theological treatises, and all other religious texts were found only in Latin. The Christian religion is based on the written word, and the basic function of Latin was summed up in the designation in the *Peterborough Chronicle*: *boc leden*, Book Latin.

Bede's *Ecclesiastical History* is the only detailed account of Britain in the seventh and early eighth centuries, and provides very valuable information about the languages of the island.

What Bede says about the general situation is almost identical to what was quoted from the *Peterborough Chronicle* above. In fact, that passage in the chronicle is more or less a condensed translation from Bede, who also asserts that five languages are used in the island. The first one is called *lingua Anglorum*, "the language of the Angles," in Latin. That corresponds of course to *Englisc* in the Chronicle. Bede obviously regarded English as one language, with a name of its own.

He also talks about written English a couple of times. In one passage, he mentions Ethelbert's law, and expressly states that it is extant and "written in the speech of the Angles," *conscripta Anglorum sermone*. He further tells a story about the first English poet, a man called Caedmon who lived in Northumbria in the later part of the seventh century. He received from heaven the gift to sing accomplished poetry in "the language of the Angles," *Anglorum lingua*, about the Christian beliefs.

Bede regarded both the poetry of Caedmon and the law of Ethelbert as compositions in English, his own native spoken language, although they were clearly in somewhat different dialects. At least from his time and onwards the uncontested view is that English in Britain is one language, which is both spoken and written.

Why was the language of the Germans named after the Angles? There is no certain answer, but actually Bede may have some role in the process leading to that result. He is the earliest author who writes extensively about the English people (which he calls *gens Anglorum*), and his words have always carried much weight. The fact that he uses the term *lingua Anglorum* several times in his historical work may not have been without importance.

Earlier Latin writers tended to use the general terms *Saxones*, "Saxons," and *Saxonia*, "Saxony," (rather than *Anglii* and *Anglia*) for the German invaders and their territory. As for Bede himself, he does not always use the same term. He talks about *lingua Anglorum* several times, both in contrast to other languages and when discussing events in Anglia and in Kent. But a couple of times, when relating events in Wessex and Essex, he calls the language *lingua Saxonum* "the language of the Saxons," and a similar designation also appears in a document he quotes. In Bede's time, it seems that it was natural to talk about the Saxon language when the Saxons used it, and the English language when it was used by Angles. But Bede lived all his life in Northumbria, and thus was an Angle himself, so it would be natural for him to use *lingua Anglorum* as the term for the language as a whole. That may be why English is now English, and not Saxon.

KING ALFRED AND WEST SAXON

For a century and a half after Bede, few people in England may have devoted themselves to writing. At any rate we possess few texts that are known to be composed during this time, in Latin or in English. These were troubled times, especially since the start of the Viking raids in the early part of the ninth century.

King Alfred the Great (871–99) initiated a new era for English literature. He was the ruler of the West Saxons, in Wessex, and was the successful leader of English resistance against the invading Danish Vikings, who had settled permanently in parts of eastern England and threatened to take control of the whole island.

In addition to his military and political feats, King Alfred found time for extensive and very important literary activities. He had learnt to read and write English early in life, and later on he acquired knowledge of Latin. This was rare: according to him there were in his time very few people south of the Humber who could translate a letter in Latin into English, and not many north of it either. An important reason for this decline of learning was no doubt that the Vikings had ravaged monasteries and churches, killing many literate people and putting an end to organized education in most places.

Alfred was a devout Christian as well as an excellent administrator, and he had seen the world: he had been to Rome at an early age. He realized how vital it was that more people learn to read. Under the circumstances, he did not find it practical to build mainly on the feeble tradition of Latin learning. Instead, he started a very ambitious programme of translations of important texts from Latin into English. Some texts he himself took on, and other people followed his example. Alfred also produced a substantial law in his own name. All in all, the number of English texts grew significantly.

Why did the king of Wessex do all this? A genuine love of letters and a strong faith, no doubt. But he also created a common literary language for the whole of England, something well in line with his political ambitions to unite the English in the fight against the Danes.

As we have seen, the few texts in English produced before Alfred's time were set down in the local dialects of the writers. This practice did not stop in his time, but most texts were indeed written in the West Saxon dialect of Wessex, and in the course of the following century that dialect assumed the role of the standard literary form, while the kingdom of Wessex grew into the dominant political power, and the descendants of Alfred finally became kings of all England.

In the last part of the tenth century, when England was comparatively peaceful and prosperous, a reform movement within the Church also resulted in a rich production of literary works in English. Most of these were homilies, saints' lives, translations of parts of the Bible, and so on. At the same time, many earlier works in English were assembled, copied, and often changed into the standard West Saxon dialect. Most of the early English texts that are still extant were in fact written or copied during these decades. Around the year 1000, then, English had a standard written form that was used in the Kingdom of England.

The English language in this early period, from the beginnings and up to 1066, is nowadays usually referred to as Old English.

The term has been avoided above, as a reminder that the users of the language could not know about our perspective. From their point of view, it was rather a recently established language in its written form, especially when compared to Latin, the much older and more prestigious learned language used within the Church.

Anyhow, the standard written language that was later to be named Old English served as the vehicle for laws and charters, for literature (mainly religious) and for some other purposes. It was used exclusively within the new English state, in competition with Latin, and the users of this written language were found mainly among the secular and religious élite of this state: the court, the noblemen, the bishops, abbots, monks, and other ecclesiastics. When the state was invaded and its leading persons removed, the standard language also disappeared.

NORMANS AND FRENCH

The Norman conquest of England entailed, among other things, a language shift among the entire leading class. After 1066, most English-speaking lords, bishops, abbots, and other important persons were ousted and/or killed, and their successors were invariably French-speaking Normans. The languages used in writing were Latin and French. French was the spoken language at court and wherever any of the new rulers were present. In this way, the two spoken languages acquired distinctive social roles. After a couple of generations, those belonging to the upper strata of society spoke mainly French, regardless of the language of their ancestors, while ordinary people still used English, and usually knew little or no French.

In this way, the role of the English language in society was drastically altered. Before the Conquest, the recently united state had been remarkably homogeneous in language usage. The Celtic languages were spoken mainly outside the state. The Danes and other Scandinavians who had moved into the country from the ninth century and onwards were no doubt largely on their way towards linguistic assimilation. So the great majority of the inhabitants of the state of England did indeed speak English. Further, as we have just seen, a written standard language was being created. But within a generation or two, the upper class spoke French, and the use of English in writing almost disappeared. English was demoted from its privileged position and became the language of the powerless.

Similar things have happened many times, and some instances have been noted above. The Romans conquered Gaul and imposed their rule, and eventually their language, on the Celts. Later on, the Germanic invaders reduced the speakers of Latin to their subjects in the same country.

As is seen by the two examples, the outcome of such a situation is not predetermined. The Romans made Latin the dominant language in most of their empire. But Latin never became a native language of Britain, and the Franks, the Burgundians, and the other Germanic invaders in Gaul lost their own language, just as the descendants of the French-speaking Normans did in England. In some cases, both languages survive in the same country. The Swedes occupied Finnish-speaking Finland in the twelfth century, and held it for about 600 years. When Swedish rule ceased in 1810, there was still only a minority of speakers of

Swedish, while the solid majority spoke Finnish. Both languages are still used in Finland today.

In England, as we know, French eventually disappeared, but for a long time that must have seemed a very unlikely development. Up to the early thirteenth century the position of French became ever more important, while the leading classes of England and France seemed to amalgamate more and more completely. The kings of England also held several duchies in France. Some of them spent most of their time there, and a few knew no or very little English. Important landowners often possessed holdings on the Continent as well as in England.

However, the fact that the king of England was also very powerful within the kingdom of France was not unproblematic. When King John of England was deprived of the duchy of Normandy in 1204, that marked the beginning of a reversal. Through a chain of political developments, the kingdoms of England and France became more and more antagonistic. Important people had to choose sides, and become either English or French. In 1337, the conflict escalated into an open fight, the Hundred Years War, which in fact dragged on to 1453, even longer than its name implies.

The political rift between England and France had no sudden linguistic effects, but in the long run the consequences became very important. The members of the leading class in England gradually lost direct, personal contacts with France in the course of the thirteenth century, as England became a political entity more and more distinct from France. Their own first language remained French for quite some time, but relations with the English-speaking common people made it necessary for most to know both languages. By and by, the English language also became more and more clearly associated with the kingdom of England. It became the spoken language in the army and in the lawcourts in the late fourteenth century, and became the main written language in administration half a century later. In the late fifteenth century, after the long war, French in effect ceased to be a native spoken language in England.

In this way English again became the main language of England. However, the situation just before 1066 was very different from that in the fifteenth century. At the time of the Norman Conquest, England had been a united kingdom for only a short time, and Danish kings had ruled over large parts of the country for centuries. The English language had constituted a cultural bond for a long time, but it had recently become the language of one state, rather than of several.

In the fifteenth century, England had been ruled by one king for more than four centuries. It was one, well-integrated country with legal and constitutional traditions of its own, with a well-defined territory that was similar to the area in which English was used. When English definitely became dominant in this country, language and state were linked more intimately than had ever been the case before the Conquest.

In fact, the ascendancy of English is one aspect of the transformation of England from a feudal kingdom to a nation-state. The subjects of the early Norman kings, in England and on the Continent, were united by the simple fact that they all had the king as their overlord, through a shorter or longer series of vassals. This feudal principle gradually broke down during the later Middle Ages, in England as well as elsewhere in Europe. In its place, there developed the idea of a state consisting of a king and his people. Ideally, each people had its own distinctive identity, with common cultural traditions, including a common language. When English triumphed over French, England came considerably closer to that ideal.

It is worthwhile to compare this change in England with what happened in other European states during this period. First, however, something about what became of the English language itself.

THE NEW ENGLISH

Very little was written in English during the first century and a half after the Norman Conquest. As we know about the language of earlier periods mainly through written sources, there is much uncertainty about what happened during that time.

From around 1200 and onwards, people wrote in English again. However, the texts were quite different from those produced before the Conquest. There was no standard language any more: the fairly uniform spelling and grammar based on West Saxon speech that dominated in the tenth and eleventh centuries had disappeared altogether. Instead, each author seemed to write and spell more or less according to his own spoken dialect. For a period of about 200 years, there were again many written dialects, just as in the earliest period of written English.

The reasons were not the same, though. In the early Anglo-Saxon period, different written forms tended to be associated with different kingdoms, and could have become competing official languages. In the thirteenth and early fourteenth centuries, there was just one state, in which the official languages were French and Latin. How to write English was not the concern of the court or of anyone in power, and the writers often addressed a small and fairly local readership.

Further, the language everywhere changed much. As has been discussed above, all languages change at all periods. However, the rate is not always the same. English was transformed rapidly during the three centuries after 1066. The general reasons for this are fairly obvious. Just as was the case with Latin in present-day France after the fall of the Roman Empire, English was dissociated from power in society, and the ruling class did not speak the language at all. Local styles of speech were not influenced by any kind of central or common norm. On the other hand, many speakers of English also used other languages, primarily French but also Latin and others.

There were important developments in grammar and vocabulary. Early English was highly inflected, which means that most words had endings. For nouns, the endings indicated singular or plural, as in modern English, where *–s* indicates plural and no ending means singular, as in *sons* and *son*. However, there were several different endings for different sets of nouns. Further, the endings also denoted case or grammatical function; the only residue of that in present-day English is the *'s* for genitive.

The verbs were also equipped with a rich inventory of endings. In the earlier quote from *Beowulf*, the form *wille* ends in *–e* because the subject is "I," and *asecgan* ends in *–an* because it is an infinitive, "to say."

This whole system of endings broke down between about 1050, when the old system was in full force, and 1350, when one finds more or less the same endings as in present-day English.

It has been discussed why English was altered so thoroughly, while other Germanic languages, such as German, still keep most of the inflections inherited from the common proto-language. Some people have asserted that this made the language easier, and more efficient and/or logical, thereby implying that languages such as German are difficult and inefficient. Modern linguists tend to deny that languages can be ranked on a scale like that, and for good reasons. Any real language is so complex that it is pointless to try to evaluate it in such a simplistic way. Besides, it should be remembered that as long as the highly inflected languages Latin and Greek were looked upon as the most perfect languages, it was axiomatic that a large number of endings is a hallmark of excellence.

It is known, however, that some inflection is often lost in languages that are subjected to strong influences from others, as we will see later, for example when discussing Afrikaans. That is certainly relevant for English. Endings were lost first in the north and in the eastern midlands, where the Danish influence was strong. That was not because Danish did not have inflection; it had. But bilingualism in the closely related languages may have caused confusion in the system, and that eventually led to its breakdown.

As for vocabulary, the influx of French and Latin words during the same period transformed English from a purely Germanic language to a language with a basic Germanic structure but with mainly non-Germanic words. Around 90 per cent of the words in an English dictionary are of French, Latin, or Greek origin. If one counts words in a text or in a recording of speech, the proportion of Germanic words is much higher, for they are the most frequent ones, while most of the loans that figure in a dictionary are learned, rare items. Still, the number of loans is extraordinary.

Two processes are involved in this massive introduction of new items. In the first place, the conquerors brought with them their own expressions and terms for very many objects and concepts, from *sovereign* to *peasant*, from *beef* to *jelly*, from *mansion* to *cabin*. This affected most areas of human activity, and there often already existed words for these or similar things in English, so that the new words were used as synonyms or to discern between closely related concepts, as *mansion* from French is partly synonymous with the old English word *house*. This kind of borrowing went on as long as there was still a French-speaking upper class in the country, that is till some time in the fifteenth century.

The second process is the introduction of learned words for new concepts. This had of course been going on before the Norman invasion, and continues up to the present day. When Augustine arrived in Kent around 600, he and his followers brought with them not only the concepts but also the words for *psalm, martyr*, and the like. But from the thirteenth century, the whole intellectual heritage from antiquity is imported into English, together with many later additions. It became possible to talk and write in English about *philosophy* as well as about *triangles*, about *medicine*, and about *paintings*. At this time, European societies became much more complex, and the new words that became necessary soon appeared in English, such as *bill* or *investiture*. As was natural, they mostly came via French, but sometimes they were taken directly from Latin, as these two examples were.

The first process is specific to English and the era of French dominance. The second one is just one small part of a much larger development, the gradual formation of a common European set of concepts for culture and science. This has been going on since the Greeks introduced such terms as *music* and *mathematics*, and the stock of words is being enlarged continually: fairly recent additions are for example *postmodernism* and the *internet*. In the period we are discussing, the English language assimilated the European inheritance by admitting thousands of words from other languages, and from that time and onwards it has partaken in the ongoing enlargement and revision of that legacy.

In sum, then, both the grammar and the vocabulary of English were substantially altered during a period of 300 years, from the mid-eleventh to the mid-fourteenth century. The earlier standard written language, West Saxon, disappeared completely, and several dialects were used in writing.

THE NEW STANDARD ENGLISH

Up to about 1350, English was hardly used at all for official purposes or in schools. But around that time it took over the role of French in some schools, and the authorities of the state introduced and encouraged it in several functions, in speech and writing.

This rather sudden change of status coincided with a rapid development in the written language. Writers became much less prone to use local dialects in writing. A common literary idiom was created in the course of a century. It had its roots mainly in the spoken language of the centre of power, London.

One important part in this development was the appearance of popular literary works of high quality, the most important being *The Canterbury Tales* by Geoffrey Chaucer, written in the 1390s. The work had much influence on later literary production, and was written in the author's east midlands dialect, very close to the language of London.

Even more important, though, may have been the evolution of written English in the Chancery. An important turning point was 1417, when Henry V shifted from French to English in his own correspondence. The king's own usage (as implemented by his clerks) probably served as an important model. Around the middle of the fifteenth century the royal bureaucrats wrote a fairly standardized language based on the London dialect. No doubt their way of writing in turn was a model for writers in many parts of the country.

Finally, the first printing office for English books was set up in London in 1476, and the printer, William Caxton, published a great number of books, mainly written in what was now a reasonably well-established standard for written English. By and large, the advent of printed texts marked the end of writing in any other dialect than the standard written language. Although there was still considerable variation in details of spelling and the like, one universally recognized norm for writing had come into existence. The norm has been gradually transformed over the centuries, but the situation is still basically the same. Any writer of English is expected to adhere to one common norm for spelling and grammar, regardless of the writer's own way of speaking the language.

NATION STATE AND NATIONAL LANGUAGE

England was not the only state in Europe in which language was very important in the formation of a nation. As a matter of fact, what happened in England is one not entirely typical instance of what came about in several parts of the Continent, from the eleventh century and onwards. A few cases have been treated already, such as the appearance of French in France and Italian in Italy. In most large European countries, there is a real national language not later than the sixteenth century, but in some areas there are similar developments much later, as will be seen. It may be appropriate to point to some common trends.

First, the new languages of Europe were both spoken and written languages, and they were written in the Latin script. Further, they competed with Latin as written languages, and in the very long perspective they have supplanted it. This of course is something quite specific for Europe during the Middle Ages. In antiquity, a strongly modified alphabet was often elaborated for a new language to be used in writing. The Latin alphabet differs considerably both from the Greek and the Etruscan one. Later ones such as the Germanic runes and the Irish ogham runes are also very different from their models. But those early innovations eventually disappeared from western Europe, and the Latin alphabet remained as the only viable script. The reason was certainly that Latin and the Latin alphabet were taught systematically in the schools of the Church, which had no strong competition.

Secondly, the success of the new written languages depended greatly on their relation to the political power. English flowered in the tenth and eleventh centuries, when King Alfred and his successors promoted it, and again from the fourteenth century, as England was being transformed into a nation state. The time in between was that of the French-speaking élite. While the majority kept their spoken language throughout the centuries, the effect of the power shift on writing was immediate and very large.

Thirdly, the names of the new languages were usually established a little later than the first appearance of the written language. This was noted for French and for Italian above, and is also true for English: the first known text is the law of Ethelbert from the early seventh century, while the name "Englisc" is attested in the ninth century (and its Latin counterpart *lingua Anglorum* in the eighth). The names are very important, as they denote written languages but at the same time also define the spoken ones.

Several such written languages appeared in Europe. Some were successful and are still well established, such as French, English, Swedish, Italian, and German. Others had their heyday, but are now decaying or gone, such as Occitan and Frisian. A few just got started, but never quite made it; the language of Gotland, the largest island in the Baltic Sea, provides an example. The only extensive document is *Gutalagen*, the law of Gotland, written in the thirteenth century. The language is a

Scandinavian one, neither quite like Danish nor quite like Swedish. If Gotland had become an independent state (which seemed quite probable at one time) this state may have developed an acknowledged independent written language. This did not happen, but the island became Swedish, and today the spoken language of the island is universally regarded as a Swedish dialect.

So a main trend in Europe from the eleventh through to the sixteenth century was that Latin, which had been more or less the universal written language, had to give way to a number of national languages, firmly established in their respective states.

Does this mean that the number of European languages became higher? That is not quite as evident as it may seem. True, all the Romance languages arose from Latin, and all the Germanic ones may have had their origin in one Proto-Germanic language. Counting from the first century AD within those two groups only, the number increased considerably, from two to more than ten. But on the other hand, in the first century AD there were several other languages in western Europe, most of which are extinct by now. Perhaps the number of languages was not reduced in that area during the first fifteen centuries AD, but it almost certainly was not enhanced.

If we restrict our attention to the last 500 years of the period, from 1000 to 1500, it is obvious that several new written languages were created and acknowledged. As for the spoken languages, that is a different matter. Even in the twelfth century, the Romance area had splintered into many dialects that diverged so much that speakers from different areas probably often could not understand each other. The same goes for the Germanic region. It is not clear whether the dialects continued to diverge at the same rate after the twelfth century. The fact that new written languages appeared and were favoured within their states may have counteracted the general trend towards divergence.

England may serve as an example. As was stated above, writers of English in the thirteenth and fourteenth centuries wrote in their own dialects. In a different political situation, several written standards might have become the result. However, with the rise of the new standard written language, the dialects ceased to be written, and instead they were probably all influenced by the new official language to some extent. The only variant which went some way towards the status of a separate language was Scots, but in the end it failed to assert itself; the connection with the political development is obvious.

Thus the strong national languages had made their appearance in the sixteenth century. The topic of the next chapter is the continued growth of those languages in Europe.

Chapter 8
The Era of National Languages

When Henry V shifted from French to English in his letters, it did not go unnoticed. It was rightly interpreted as one among several ways for the king, intent on the struggle against France, to propagate the idea of a strong and independent English nation. This can be seen clearly in an often-quoted decision by the Brewers' Guild in London in 1422:

Whereas our mother-tongue, to wit the English tongue, hath in modern days begun to be honourably enlarged and adorned, for that our most excellent lord, King Henry V, hath in his letters missive and diverse affairs touching his own person, more willingly chosen to declare the secrets of his will, and for the better understanding of his people, hath with a diligent mind procured the common idiom (setting aside others) to be commended by the exercise of writing; and there are many of our craft of Brewers who have the knowledge of writing and reading in the said English idiom, but in others, to wit, the Latin and French, before these times used, they did not in any way understand. For which causes with many others, it being considered how that the greater part of the

Lords and trusty Commons have begun to make their matters be noted down in our mother tongue, so we also in our craft, following in some manner their steps, have decreed to commit to memory the needful things which concern us . . .

Both the king's language shift and the reaction of the brewers were parts of a major development that was in no way restricted to Britain. Henry V was but one of many nation builders in Europe. Persons and actions vary from country to country, but the different chains of events had surprising similarities. Various things happened at different points in time. Kings and leaders started wars or formed alliances, split up some territories and amalgamated others. Peoples revolted, prevailed or were suppressed. Still, in a long perspective it can be seen that the same thing occurred all over Europe, starting in the tenth and ending in the nineteenth century. There disappeared a large number of small states, in which the spoken language was more often than not the same as in the neighbouring states, and the written language was Latin. In their place there arose a much smaller number of states, each one with a national language of its own, spoken by most people and used officially in writing. Briefly, the nation-states were born.

England followed an unusually tortuous path, as has been described above. The small separate states were united as early as the eleventh century, but as a result of the Norman Conquest the appearance of a real national language was delayed by several hundred years. Elsewhere, the succession of events was more straightforward. In the Iberian Peninsula, for example, there were eight separate states in the year 1200. In the south, the rulers were the Muslim Almohads, who also governed the better part of northern Africa. The northern part of the peninsula was split up into several political units: Portugal (which was much smaller than now), Galicia, Asturias, León, Castile, Navarra, and Aragón. Various Iberoromance dialects or languages were spoken in the respective states, but the written language was almost exclusively Latin, and of course Arabic in the south. Four hundred years later, in 1600, Portugal and Spain had almost the same boundaries they have today. Further, the two written languages Portuguese and Castilian, also called Spanish, had been established and had become dominant in the two countries. On the other hand, the main language of Aragón, Catalan, had a very subordinate position (but has experienced a remarkable recent revival).

Here, a full discussion of all countries is out of the question. Instead, I will take up a few important aspects. The new national languages did not just spring up spontaneously, they were deliberately created. The spoken forms were often there when the new states came into existence, but the important thing was to obtain what was perceived (and is still perceived) as a real language, that is a written language with norms of its own, preferably of high status. Two of the ways towards this goal was to introduce the language in school education and to encourage authors to write in the language.

STATE, SCHOOL, AND LANGUAGES

Who invented schools for children is not known to me, but the Greeks and Romans had institutions that were partly similar to ours. Greek children had to learn to read and write just in their own language, but better-class children in Rome had to master both Latin and Greek, the two official languages of the empire.

After the fall of the Roman Empire in the west, the Christian Church was in charge of systematic education. Up to the ninth century, the schools that were found in some monasteries and cathedrals were very modest, but later on education expanded greatly, and in the twelfth century the first European universities were formed. The language in school was Latin. Since Latin was no longer anyone's native language much time in school was spent on learning the language itself, at the same time as one learnt to read and write. Those who advanced to higher studies also had to attain a good oral command of the language. Higher education was given in Latin only, and Latin had to be used in international contacts.

When the spoken languages became new written languages people were needed who could read and write them. However, for several hundred years this seems to have been arranged informally, without any changes in the school curricula. The new written languages were not used or taught in schools for a very long time.

There are isolated reports about such education as early as the thirteenth century, but it seems to have occurred only under special circumstances. There are almost no traces of schoolbooks such as readers, grammars, or dictionaries for the new languages until well into the sixteenth century. Those who wanted to read and write in the new languages had to choose one of two ways. They could learn it without any help from the schools of the Church. Some children of well-to-do parents may have done that, as they could get help from relatives and from private teachers. The other way was to learn to read and write in the native language after having mastered the same thing for Latin in school. Reading and writing are skills that may be transferred from one language to another, to a large extent at least.

As the new languages were used more and more frequently in contracts, in correspondence, and in various official contexts, school education started in the fourteenth and fifteenth centuries. However, the real breakthrough was connected with the Reformation movement in northern Europe. One of the novel ideas of that movement was that the clergy should preach the Christian faith in the languages spoken by the people, and that the central texts should be available in those languages. For a long time, the Catholic Church resisted this and stuck to Latin. Thus, the religious dispute also was a fight between languages. An early example is John Wycliff's plea for English in the fourteenth century; later reformers such as Luther and Zwingli had similar views.

The rulers of northern countries such as England, Denmark, and Sweden all saw the advantages of a Church loyal to the king rather than to the pope. Henry VIII of England, for example, decided to make the change because the pope opposed one of his divorces. When reformation was proclaimed from above in those countries the national languages also benefited. Because the gospel was to be preached and the Bible read in English, as in Danish and Swedish, those languages had to become fully established written languages, comparable to Latin.

However, Latin was not disfavoured or much reduced in importance. Kings as well as reformers took it for granted that Latin would remain the language of the educated. Luther, for one, pleaded for German in school as well as in the churches in his early days, but later on he veered towards Latin.

Thus, the countries did not switch directly from Latin to the new languages. Rather, the new languages became established as written languages as well as spoken ones, as we have discussed in some detail for English. They had not yet reached the level of Latin, but they were seen as possible alternatives. Still, this was a very important step, and the subsequent story, from the sixteenth century and onwards, records the retreat of Latin from one domain of use after another, until it ceases entirely to function as a means of linguistic communication. But that did not actually happen until the 1960s, when the Second Vatican Council decided to permit the use of other languages than Latin in the liturgy. Thereby, the need for active mastery of the language disappeared even for priests, and as a consequence Latin has now lost its role as the international language within the Catholic Church.

The new languages were still not much used in schools in the sixteenth century, but the groundwork was started. For language instruction there had to be a well-defined norm. The pupils had to learn to spell and to express themselves correctly, and so there had to be rules of orthography and grammars, and preferably dictionaries. For Latin, all this had existed for a very long time.

For the new written languages of Europe those aids were developed mainly during the sixteenth and seventeenth centuries. The first Spanish grammar appeared as early as 1492, and within a few decades there existed grammatical descriptions of French and Italian too. In the sixteenth century there appeared unpretentious grammars for foreign learners of English; the first monolingual dictionary of English was published in 1604.

In the seventeenth century, the national languages entered into real competition with Latin as the first school language and the official language. The European states were growing ever stronger, and ever more centralized. Kings and other rulers became more inclined to support the national language against Latin, which was more and more clearly associated with the Catholic Church, as the use of the language gradually diminished in other domains.

An important fact was that the states managed most of their administration in the national languages. Examples are tax collection, bookkeeping, correspondence, and so on. Stronger states required more such work, and so there was a need for people who were able to read and write documents of various kinds at many stations in society. It was no longer enough to educate the clergy, who had for several centuries constituted the bulk of literate persons.

Still, the schools did not adapt rapidly to the new situation. The realm of schools is extremely conservative, and in several countries Latin remained the main subject for centuries. In England the need for instruction in English was felt at an early stage, and several reformers advocated a more important role for it in the sixteenth and seventeenth centuries. In particular, the Puritans were in favour of this, but Latin continued to dominate the curriculum for a long time, especially at the more advanced levels.

However, it is also possible to see the development in a slightly different perspective. The traditional grammar school with

Latin, and sometimes Greek, survived for a very long time, but the new national languages took over the new areas for education. In the first place, more people received elementary education, learning to read and write, and this was almost always carried out in the national language. Secondly, there was a growing need for some theoretical education in practically oriented professions, and the national languages were chosen there too. This was true particularly for commerce and business. Another example is the military profession, which was pursued by many members of the leading class. In the seventeenth century a number of European countries set up so-called knights' schools in order to provide young noblemen with what they needed to know in their future military career. The language used was the national one, not Latin.

As Latin retreated and other languages advanced, it became necessary to know the languages of other countries in order to be able to travel and communicate with people abroad. Organized school education in French for Englishmen, in German for Swedes, and so on, started in the seventeenth century. To begin with this was important mainly for a small group of highly placed persons and diplomats, but as time went on some instruction in modern foreign languages became a normal part of school curricula in many countries.

The net effect of all this was that the new national languages of Europe caught up with Latin and eventually surpassed it in one field of activity after another. The new languages gradually took on the roles of Latin. Latin was a written language, and the script was the Latin alphabet; that was true for the new languages too. Latin had strict rules for grammar and spelling, and the national languages acquired such rules. Latin was an important school subject, and eventually the new languages assumed that function too.

NATIONAL LANGUAGES AND NATIONAL POETS

A major asset of Latin was the fact that it had a classical literature. Virgil, Cicero, and the other great Roman authors were read in school, and those who had aspirations to be persons of culture had to know them. This remained so for a long time. But the prestige of the new languages was growing, new literary works were created, and one language after another got national authors, famous writers to be studied in school just like the Latin ones. New gods replaced the old.

We have already discussed the first European national author after the Roman ones. Dante, who composed his works in the early fourteenth century, is the first important figure in a unique Italian literary tradition. Two great writers followed closely in his steps, the poet Petrarch and the prose writer Boccaccio. Those three masters of the Italian language were read, admired, and soon also commented upon, in the same way as was done with Latin texts. As an example, Boccaccio devoted himself to writing commentaries to Dante's works. The Italian language obtained its classics long before any other European national language.

In the other Romance countries there are no authors of comparable dignity for several hundred years, in spite of the fact that French was a literary language before Italian. Very important authors such as Rabelais and Montaigne appeared as late as the sixteenth century. But even though both these were much admired and much read, neither of them acquired the status of becoming a school model for language and style. That prize went to the playwrights of the seventeenth century, the tragedians Corneille and Racine and the comedy writer Molière. Their language and their ways of expression were seen as models, and their works have figured prominently in French education for centuries.

In Spain, the first great flowering of literature was at the end of the sixteenth and beginning of the seventeenth centuries. This was the time of the playwrights Calderón and Lope de Vega, and when Cervantes composed his famous satire of romances of chivalry, *Don Quixote*.

England has already been mentioned. Chaucer was an important early writer in a national language; however, he was overshadowed by the first very great and internationally famous writer in the English language, William Shakespeare, who was active at the end of the sixteenth and beginning of the seventeenth century.

Thus, France, Spain, and England saw the first great masterpieces in their own languages within less than a century, approximately between 1590 and 1670. This is no accident. The three states all gained momentum, both in political and in economic terms, and they all claimed a leading position in Europe. The authors were connected in various ways with the leaders of the states at the powerful and growing royal courts in the three dynamic capitals: Paris, Madrid, and London. As has often been the case, literary creativity flourished not far from money and power.

Writers in the different countries were of course also in contact with each other. No country developed in isolation; there were numerous connections through various channels. There was also competition between the countries of Europe in the sphere of culture, just as they competed economically and fought with each other in recurring wars.

In the other countries of Europe national literatures developed considerably later. Conditions were different, and in most countries much less favourable. As was just hinted, power and wealth are not unimportant for the formation of a new literature. But it is hardly possible for great works of art to emerge out of nowhere, even if there is much money around. There has to be a literary tradition and literary circles. Authors do depend on predecessors. Before Shakespeare there were a number of good, but now largely forgotten, Renaissance playwrights in English. Corneille and Racine could build both on French forerunners and on Spanish models.

Accordingly, the literary development in such countries as Sweden or the Netherlands was less impressive. All the same, the trends were similar to those in the larger countries. The national languages were given much attention. In Sweden, for example, the political leaders, including the kings, were strongly in favour of Swedish from the Reformation in the early sixteenth century onwards. However, little was in fact written in the language for quite some time. For a couple of centuries, the most important linguistic model remained the translation of the Bible, published in 1541. Gradually, a literature in Swedish came into existence, but no Swedish authors gained international reputation before Strindberg and Lagerlöf in the late nineteenth century.

So it was far from all European states that were able to produce impressive national authors at an early stage. All tried their best, though. The national states favoured their languages, and more so as time passed. The national language grew ever more important, and the national literature had a significant part to play. It helped in moulding the language into a fully adequate instrument for all kinds of human communication. Also, the texts of the most famous authors were used in school education. That was of great symbolic importance, especially in relation to the classical languages. Only when a language could supply literary texts of its own for use in education was it possible to begin thinking about it as comparable to Latin and Greek.

LANGUAGE AND POLITICS

The modern European languages competed with Latin in more ways than by creating national literature. The question of languages was intimately related to Europe's perception of its own cultural achievement.

The main current of ideas in the fifteenth and sixteenth centuries is the one usually subsumed under the name of the Renaissance. It included the notion that the culture of classical antiquity was exemplary, and that it should be imitated and emulated. In the field of languages, this meant that Greek became an object of serious study in western Europe, but above all that it was considered extremely important to cultivate the use of Latin. The classical authors became models to a much larger extent than previously, which created problems, as it is no easy matter to write in the style of Cicero or Virgil. A large number of Renaissance authors spent their time writing new works of art in Latin. A few are of high quality, but the readership was probably quite limited even at the time, and they have all been long forgotten except by a small number of specialists.

In the seventeenth century the central idea of the Renaissance met with serious opposition; it was proposed by some that the modern period actually surpasses antiquity. This discussion was carried on in learned circles for a couple of centuries. The most famous episode is a quarrel that started in France as late as the 1680s; it is called *la querelle des anciens et des modernes*, "the quarrel between the ancients and the moderns." A poet by the name of Perrault started the row by asserting that his own country and time, France under Louis XIV, was more distinguished than any period in antiquity. The idea met with fierce opposition from the traditionalists, but the struggle itself really was a sure sign that the domination of antiquity in Europe was coming to an end. In terms of languages, this meant mainly that Latin was losing ground in a serious way.

Louis XIV and his era were central in that development. France was the leading political and cultural force of Europe in the late seventeenth and the better part of the subsequent century. An important consequence of the dominance of France was that for people of consequence anywhere in Europe it became ever more important to know French. There were several reasons. First, there was the need to be cultured, what one may call the snob value. It became more important to have read Racine and Boileau than to know Virgil by heart. Secondly, one had to know French manners. The French court was a model for all the courts of Europe, and one had to know how to behave and how to conduct a conversation in the French style. Thirdly, a more practical aspect was that French was becoming the language of diplomacy and international contacts in general.

Up to the sixteenth century, Latin had been the only language for official international relations in Europe. However, as the leaders of national states acquired more lofty ideas about their countries and languages, attempts were made to use those languages internationally. To begin with such ideas were frowned upon as breaches of etiquette, but the situation changed when all parties knew French better than they knew Latin. As late as 1660 all discussions were conducted in Latin when a peace was negotiated in Oliva between Sweden, Austria, and Poland. But in Nijmegen in 1678, when Spain, France, Sweden, and others participated, discussions and minutes were in French, and only the peace treaty itself was drawn up in Latin. The agreement of Rastadt between Austria and France in 1714 was documented only in French, and that set the model for the future. In that way French appropriated one of the very central functions of Latin in Europe.

This was no sudden reversal, but the fruit of determined efforts over a long period. The French language had been supported, regulated, and favoured in all ways in its home country. It had grown stronger in comparison to Latin, and had also gained ground from Occitan in southern France and from other regional languages and dialects. As early as 1635, the king founded the *Académie française*, which has the task of cultivating and furthering the French language.

In sum, French first became a real national language for the successful nation-state of France, and later, as a result of the prestige and power of the state, the language advanced to a higher level, encroaching on the position of Latin as the international language.

Only one national language could aspire to reach that level, or at least only one at a time. However, ambitions in several other countries were just as high, and they launched their respective languages as best they could.

THE LANGUAGE COMPETITION

As has been shown above, a number of languages appeared in Europe in the Middle Ages. To begin with they were just spoken languages without names and without any reputation. Later on they became written languages and received names of their own, such as English, French, Italian, and Swedish. The most successful languages were associated with a state and gained the position of national languages.

There is nothing in the nature of human languages that makes such a sequence of events necessary or natural. Certainly most languages that have existed have been only spoken languages, used by small groups. Written languages and associations between languages and large states first appeared around 5,000 years ago, as was discussed above.

What is special about Europe's linguistic history is that the written language of antiquity, Latin, remained in use in western Europe for about a millennium after the fall of the western Roman Empire. The last emperor was deposed in 476, and the new languages ousted Latin as a written language in a process that stretched from around 1300 to around 1700.

Still, the new languages did not become quite what Latin had been. It is true that they were languages of powerful states, that they came to be used for all purposes in speech and writing, and that some of them became vehicles for great literature. But in contrast to Latin, they had competition.

At the earliest stage Latin was just one among several languages of Italy, but after a few centuries it actually was without rivals. Greek was and remained important, to be sure, but the Romans wielded political power also over the speakers of Greek, and in the western part of the empire Latin was totally dominant, in culture and religion as well as in politics. Its position was unthreatened, and remained so for a long time.

The modern European languages have never been in that position. They developed as written languages and languages of political power during the same period in adjacent regions, with much mutual influence. At different periods, areas of Europe ceased to be assemblies of small states with similar spoken languages and were transformed into nations with one leadership and one spoken and written language. But no state was able to rule all the others, and western Europe became an assembly of nation-states in perpetual competition in the arenas of politics, culture, and language.

In each country there was competition between the national language and Latin, as we have seen. The nation's language gradually intruded into the various domains of the traditional written language. Parts of the development could be swift, but in general the process was quite slow. More than a millennium elapsed from the first use of English for legal texts around AD 600 to the abolition of Latin as an official language in Hungary in the mid-nineteenth century. Latin was pitted against the national languages in a contest that finally led to the demise of Latin, but also moulded the new written languages into a certain similarity with the old one.

This process has been alluded to in the discussion of English above. Not only English, but all other European languages have imported a vast number of words from written Latin during the Middle Ages and later. This is true also for the Romance languages, which originate from Latin to begin with. To illustrate this, take the word *popular*, first attested in English in the sixteenth century. It originates from the Latin adjective *popularis*, which is derived from the noun *populus*, "people." The word is found in most European languages: *populär* in German and Swedish, *popolare* in Italian, *populaire* in French, and so on. The French word cannot have existed in the French language from the beginning, for in that case it would not be so similar to the Latin form. The Latin *populus* has been in French all the time, and has been transformed to *peuple*. If *popularis* had been through the same development it would probably have ended up as *peupler*. Therefore, French must have imported the adjective *populaire* from written Latin.

The many competing languages of Europe have incessantly borrowed words and expressions from each other. Latin and Greek provided many of the stems, as we have seen, but of course it also happened that one of the languages created an appropriate word, which was then taken over in all the other ones. The weapon called *musket* in English was first given the name *moschetto*, "small fly," in Italian. The weapon became popular over all of Europe, and the name travelled with the object; it was borrowed into each language with minor phonetic variations.

The leaders in the fight for the new languages were almost always people not far from the central power in the state. The new languages are often called popular languages, as opposed to Latin, the language of learning and the learned, but as a matter of fact this designation is hardly appropriate. As written languages and school languages the new languages were the creations of the masters, not of the people. To be sure they were more acceptable among ordinary people than Latin was, as they were based on what people in general actually spoke. But the written standard forms of French or English did not reflect how average speakers used the language but rather how it was used in the court and among the noblemen.

The new languages were written languages, and they had to be propagated through systematic education and training. It took a very long time before they had fully penetrated the system of education. Latin remained strong in the schools of most European countries throughout the nineteenth century, while the new languages slowly wormed their way into the curricula. To begin with they were used only for elementary reading and writing, later on for arithmetic, and still later literary texts were introduced. For difficult matters such as science, philosophy, and religion, Latin was necessary up to a century and a half ago.

Emulation of the other national languages was even more important than competition with Latin. The standing of the national language had a lot to do with the import of the nation state. For centuries there was rivalry between English and French, just as there was between England and France. Portuguese vied with Spanish, and Swedish was the emblem of the state of Sweden, in perpetual contest with Danish and Denmark. By and large (though not without exceptions), the European states that maintained their political independence also managed to uphold their national languages and make them prevail within their territories.

In that way, linguistic unities gradually became more and more coterminous with political unities. The last great step in that direction was when Germany and Italy became nation-states around the middle of the nineteenth century, and the situation has not changed much since then. Europe consists mostly of nation-states, each with a national language, and because of a long period of European predominance, this has set a model for much of the world.

Chapter 9

Languages of Europe and of the World

On 9 March in the year 1500, a naval expedition set sail and left the port of Lisbon. The goal was to repeat the performance of Vasco da Gama two years earlier, sailing round Africa to reach India. Pedro Cabral, the leader of the expedition, steered far south-west in the Atlantic, in order to avoid the doldrums outside the Gulf of Guinea. On 22 April he reached a shore, which he thought was part of an island, and he named it the True Cross, *Vera Cruz*. He was wrong, however, for he had found a continent. Cabral and his followers were the first Europeans to set foot in Brazil.

The arrival of the Portuguese in South America was not entirely accidental. A few years before, Columbus had proved that there was land westwards, across the Atlantic, and the coast of South America had been seen from ships before Cabral set out. For that reason it was natural that he made an extra turn in that direction just to find out what might be there. Curiosity was hardly the main reason. As a matter of fact, Portugal had already acquired sovereignty over this land in the west, provided that it existed.

When the Portuguese sailor Diaz had travelled beyond the Cape of Good Hope in 1488, and Columbus had been to the West Indies in 1492 on behalf of the Spanish crown, leading circles in Europe realized that great things were in the making. Trade amounting to fabulous sums was at stake, and possibly rule over large countries. There was so much to gain that the situation could easily take a dangerous turn, as the states of Europe might go to war over the booty. That was why the two leading naval powers, Spain and Portugal, decided to share the world outside Europe between them. In the Treaty of Tordesillas of 1494, it was agreed that Spain was to have everything west of a certain longitude, between 48 and 49 degrees west of the Greenwich meridian. Whatever was east of that line would go to Portugal.

Now, eastern Brazil happens to be east of the demarcation line. Cabral was keenly aware of that, and he declared that the land he had found belonged to the king of Portugal. The fact that it was already inhabited by people he met was irrelevant in his view. In the European perspective, Brazil was under Portuguese rule before a single Portuguese had actually been there.

Portugal did not succeed in subduing the world outside Europe east of the 48 degrees western longitude. Besides, a weakness of the Treaty was that the demarcation line on the other side of the globe was never specified. But for South America, the Treaty of Tordesillas was decisive. In accordance with it, Portugal occupied the eastern part of the continent and

Spain took everything else. That is why Portuguese is the language of Brazil, while Spanish predominates in almost all the other states of America south of the United States.

The language shifts in America from the fifteenth century and onwards are some of the most important linguistic changes in world history. At the same time, there are violent changes in population. The history of Brazil is typical. At the time when the Portuguese arrived there may have been a few million people in the enormous area which now constitutes that country, about 90 times the size of Portugal. Those people spoke a very large number of languages. No one knows how many, but in the whole of South America there are still around 350 American Indian languages, although many of those spoken around 1500 are certainly gone. It seems safe to assume that there were hundreds of languages in Brazil alone. Many people who lived there were gatherers, hunters, and fishermen, but there was also some farming.

The Portuguese first settled along the coast and of course procured their food through farming of the European type. This will feed many more people per square kilometre than gathering and hunting, as has already been discussed. Within a few hundred years there were more descendants of Portuguese than there had been people in the country when they arrived. In addition, the Portuguese imported many slaves from Africa, and the original Indian population became more and more integrated into the Portuguese society. The eventual result was a large population of mixed genetic origin with one common language, Portuguese. This population is still growing; at present the number of inhabitants of Brazil is around 160 million. The native language is Portuguese for all except groups of Indians in isolated parts of the Amazon region.

This is partly similar to what happened when speakers of Bantu languages took over large parts of Africa a couple of thousand years ago. The number of people grew rapidly, and there was a massive language shift. But there is also a great difference. When the various groups of Bantu speakers dispersed in different directions their languages soon diversified, and there are now hundreds of Bantu languages. There is no such development in Brazil. It is true that Brazilian Portuguese is now not entirely similar to the language spoken in Portugal, but the two variants are mutually comprehensible without difficulty (in most cases).

The reason is of course that the Portuguese were disposed to preserve political and linguistic unity. There was a colonial government, which was succeeded in the beginning of the nineteenth century by the central authorities of the independent state of Brazil. There was a state administration, a school system, and an army. All used Portuguese as their spoken language, and those who wanted to make a career in society had to use the written language that was and is the same as in Portugal.

SPANIARDS, ENGLISHMEN, AND THE OTHERS

A few decades after Columbus's first journey in 1492 it became evident that the country in the west is not the eastern part of Asia but a continent of its own. This became fully clear only when the companions of Magalhães (Magellan) completed a circumnavigation of the globe in 1520–2. By then, the Europeans had already started their systematic hunt for riches and fertile land in the unknown territories.

The Spaniards occupied the whole of Central and South America except for Brazil. They behaved as ruthless conquerors. In a couple of places they encountered important states that they overturned and destroyed with brutal swiftness. A well-known episode is when the adventurer Pizarro managed to topple the huge Inca Empire on the west coast of South America with less than 200 soldiers and 30 horses. The loot was mainly large quantities of gold.

The Spaniards also crushed the Maya culture in Central America, where a wholly original writing system of the hieroglyphic type had been in use. The remaining inscriptions and manuscripts, which are not very numerous, have been deciphered only in the last decades. Thus it has not become clear until quite recently that this was a fully developed written language. This is important for several reasons, one of them being that the art of writing was almost certainly invented at least twice quite independently. The alternative is to assume some otherwise unattested early contacts between Central America and Asia or Europe. Anyhow, this writing system sank into oblivion.

The Spanish invasion started as mere plundering but gradually grew into something much more important. The Spaniards stayed in the conquered territories. People moved there from Europe and became farmers and businessmen. Towns were founded quite early. The Spanish state created a bureaucracy to handle the large expanses of land that now came under the jurisdiction of the king of Spain.

At a fairly early stage the king appointed viceroys who acted as governors over large regions. In the eighteenth century there were four viceroyalties: Rio de la Plata (present Chile, Bolivia, Argentina, etc.), Peru (Peru, Ecuador), New Granada (Colombia, Venezuela), New Spain (Central America, Mexico, south-western United States). It was no easy matter to keep together this vast empire, sparsely populated and lacking good internal communications.

At the beginning of the nineteenth century all the territories on the continent divested themselves from Spanish rule. After a complex series of splits the situation became what it is now. In America Spanish is the official language in eighteen independent states, from Mexico in the north to Chile in the south. In addition, around 15 per cent of the population of the United States use Spanish as their first language. Altogether, Spanish is the native language of more than 300 million people in America. Spain has a total population of about 40 million, and the number of native speakers of Spanish is smaller, for some use Catalan or Basque as their first language.

Spanish gained its position in most American countries more or less as Portuguese did in Brazil, and for similar reasons. The conquest itself was not decisive, for countries have often been conquered without any language shift. Spaniards moved to America in fairly large numbers. Their administration was efficient, comparatively speaking, and they had a written language. They also succeeded in breaking down and destroying the existing large states. The indigenous population that was not large to begin with dwindled fast, partly at least because of smallpox and other diseases that spread from the Europeans. In a few generations the speakers of Spanish were a sizeable minority, in possession of all political power.

In this situation, many speakers of Indian languages shifted to Spanish, for economic and political reasons. At present several hundred Indian languages are still used, but the number of speakers is low for all except a few, as Quechua and Aymara in Peru, Bolivia, and Argentina.

In terms of numbers of people as well as numbers of languages, the transition to Spanish in America is probably the largest linguistic change in history. When the Spaniards arrived about 50 million people used several hundred languages. Now, 300 million speak the same language.

The Spanish and the Portuguese were the first Europeans who travelled great distances in order to subjugate the world, but others were not far behind. Several states realized that long-distance trade and conquests could be very lucrative. From the beginning of the seventeenth century the political history of the world has much to do with claims and possessions of European states in various parts of the world.

In the eastern part of North America there was a regular race for colonies; the participants were England, France, the Netherlands, and Sweden. Each state introduced its own language. Dutch and Swedish soon disappeared, but English was remarkably successful. The earliest British immigrants arrived in the 1620s, and as is well known, the colonies liberated themselves from British sovereignty as early as 1776. At that time there was already a sizeable English-speaking population, and it was growing fast. In 1790, there were 4 million. But the great expansion took place in the nineteenth century, when the United

States expanded westwards and multiplied its population several times, largely through immigration from Europe.

As a result, North America is now populated by about 280 million people in the United States and Canada. The original inhabitants, Indians and Inuits, have not disappeared but are now just quite small minorities, and their languages are almost all on their way to extinction, if they have not already vanished. The immigrants from all countries of Europe and from several parts of Asia have not produced a multilingual society; almost all speak English. The early colonies of France have also left a linguistic imprint in that around 6 million people in Quebec in Canada use French as their first language.

There is also an important recent development that should be mentioned. Because of massive immigration in the last three or four decades from several American countries, there are now in the United States at least 30 million people whose first language is Spanish.

It would be incorrect to contend that Britain as a colonial power promoted English to become the main language of North America. Britain has had no political mandate in America for more than two centuries, and at that time the English-speaking population was just about 1 per cent of what it is now.

Rather, what happened was a huge movement of people from Europe and Africa to North America and an explosive population growth. English became the language of the new country as the first and most influential colonists had their roots in Britain, and the United States accordingly used English as the common, national language. The remarkable thing is that the immigrants shifted to English with so few exceptions. Large groups from several countries kept their languages for a generation or two, but now almost all descendants of those immigrants use English.

The shifts certainly often had to do with economy and careers. However, in other countries such considerations have not prevented linguistic minorities from retaining their language for many generations. For the European immigrants and their children, it was probably even more important that they strongly wished to identify with the new country and its values. They chose America for life when they left Italy or Poland or Sweden, and their primary interest was to succeed in the new country, not to maintain the links to the old one. They shifted to English in order to become true Americans.

The ones who came from Africa had a very different lot. They were imported as slaves, and were deprived of their native languages, as will be discussed below. English was imposed upon them, rather than chosen. They could not hope for social or economic advancement, and as a consequence their use of language tended to create a separate identity rather than to integrate them into a hostile society. This is one of the reasons why many Americans of African descent still speak in a way that differs markedly from the official norm.

It seems that the latest immigrants to the United States may be the first ones to assert their own linguistic identity in the long run. The speakers of Spanish from American countries are not being assimilated as the European immigrants were, nor are they suppressed in the way the African slaves were. Further, their homelands are much closer, and with modern communications it is comparatively easy to keep in touch. For the first time,

English has some competition in the United States. This is most clearly shown by the fact that a large number of the states of the union have legislated in favour of English in recent years. There has not been any need for that before.

But in the large perspective, that is a minor redistribution of two European languages on the American continent. The main trend in the development is clear enough.

AMERICA—A CONTINENT WITH THREE LANGUAGES

In 500 years, the population of the American continent has multiplied several times, and most people who live there now speak one of only three languages: Portuguese, Spanish, or English. Linguistically, this is unique in world history. Nothing like it has occurred before, nor will it happen again, for it came about as people in possession of a new technology overpowered others without that technology and took control of a large swathe of the surface of earth. The Europeans had sailing ships, guns, horses, and ploughs. The ships took them to America, with the guns they conquered the inhabitants, and agriculture helped them multiply and replenish the new earth.

They also had their languages. When the Europeans started their conquests in the sixteenth century these languages had not very long histories as written national languages. All three—Portuguese, Spanish, and English—still vied with Latin in official contexts. The great national authors as well as the detailed norms for spelling and style emerged in the sixteenth and seventeenth centuries. However, in the conquered lands in America

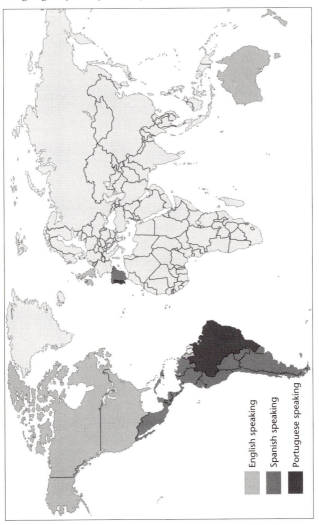

MAP 6. Parts of the world in which the native first language is predominantly European

English speaking
Spanish speaking
Portuguese speaking

the European national languages had the upper hand from the beginning. With few exceptions, the indigenous languages were neglected or repressed. To have one common language is a characteristic of most American states, and that has been so for a long time.

At present the population of the American continent is around 700 million people, or approximately as many as in Europe. In Europe there are around thirty states and almost as many national languages, each spoken by at least a few million speakers. The number of states in America is about the same (if the West Indies are included), but there are just three large languages, and only five with more than a couple of million speakers, namely Spanish, English, Portuguese, Quechua, and French. A few other languages enjoy an official position, namely Dutch in Surinam (formerly Dutch Guyana) and Haitian in Haiti.

So Europe has around thirty national languages, America in practice has three, while the number of people is about the same. It can be said, of course, that the reason was that three European powers were the conquerors. But that is not a sufficient explanation, for earlier migrations and conquests rarely had such results. The Europeans were fairly numerous in comparison with the original inhabitants, and these were severely decimated through epidemic diseases introduced from Europe, while the Europeans multiplied through an unusually high reproduction rate. Further, they did not develop new language forms that deviated from the original European languages. This occurred elsewhere, as we will see, but almost not at all on the American mainland. Written language and schools existed from the beginning, and the ties with the European languages were strong enough to prevent splits. For these reasons the linguistic situation of America changed from very fragmented to very homogeneous.

Although the three large languages keep in touch with the mother languages in Europe, some differences have of course developed between American and European usage. The most important ones concern pronunciation. An American does not sound like an Englishman, and a Mexican does not speak quite like a Spaniard. But these are fairly moderate dialectal differences, and in fact the variants cannot always be easily classified as American versus European. For example, in standard American English pronunciation an *r* sound is heard at the end of words like *four* and *father*, but in standard British pronunciation there is no such sound. But in fact the *r* is present in many dialects of the British Isles, while it is absent in some eastern American dialects. There are of course also some more clear-cut differences, for example in spelling and vocabulary, but on the whole the American languages have retained their identity with their European counterparts.

PORTUGAL AND THE REST OF THE WORLD

For Pedro Cabral, the visit to Brazil really was just a detour. His main task was to establish business relations with India, and he was successful. Many others followed suit, and throughout the sixteenth century Portugal controlled the seas from Gibraltar to China, travelling between numerous harbours and trading posts.

In some areas the Portuguese also took hold of extensive stretches of land along the coasts. Three of them were Portuguese colonies for a very long time but are now independent African states, namely Guinea-Bissau, Angola, and Mozambique. In these three states the Portuguese language still has a very strong position as official language and language of the schools. All the same, the situation is quite different from that in Brazil. In the African countries Portuguese has never become the first language for more than a few per cent of the population. Most people still speak one of the many languages that existed in the countries before the arrival of the Portuguese.

It is not very difficult to guess the reason. The Portuguese probably behaved in Africa more or less as they did in America, but conditions were not the same. The decisive factor was population. There were probably more people in Africa, at least in relation to the land available for farming. Further, the Africans did not succumb to epidemics in the way the American Indians did, doubtless because the diseases of Europe were not entirely new to the African continent. There was no place for a new population to rise and multiply fast.

So Portuguese in America developed into a native tongue, but Portuguese in Africa became a colonial language. Such a language is used by the officials of a colonial power to govern the colony, and it often acquires an important position in the schools, in administration, and in the economy in general. It may keep that position even when the colony has gained political independence. In the former Portuguese colonies in Africa, the Portuguese language is still the official language, the language of instruction in schools and the main language for international contacts.

In Asia the Portuguese did not occupy any large areas, although it was the primary target of their expansion. They acquired fortified trading posts, two of which have remained Portuguese until the later part of the twentieth century, Goa in India (united with India in 1961) and Macao in China (united with China in 1999). Linguistically speaking, they were of no great importance. Portuguese is still spoken in Macao, but everyone also understands Cantonese Chinese.

Still, the overall result of Portugal's period of conquest was that in a few hundred years, Portuguese was transformed from just a European language, spoken by perhaps a million people, to one of the great languages of the world, the native tongue of almost 200 million people. In terms of numbers, this is comparable to how Latin spread in antiquity and how Arabic expanded in the Middle Ages. Still, Portugal was just one of the European colonial powers, and not the most successful one.

ENGLISH OVERSEAS

The other colonial powers looked for land and riches in the East, just like Portugal, and some had great success. In southern Asia Britain made India and several other areas parts of its empire. The Dutch colonized the whole of what is now Indonesia, and the French laid their hands on what was called Indochina, the present-day states of Cambodia, Laos, and Vietnam. The European languages were important colonial languages, and English still has a very significant role in India. Still, the colonies in Asia did not give rise to large populations speaking European languages. The countries were comparatively densely populated already, and in several areas there were languages with many speakers that had also been used in writing for a very long time.

Britain exploited the last remaining continent, Australia. In some ways the situation there resembled that of North America. The native people did not farm, and as a consequence they were not very numerous. However, for climatic reasons the country was less tempting. It became known to Europeans at the beginning of the seventeenth century, but there was no invasion until much later. Through the Declaration of Independence in 1776 Britain lost its colonies in the west and started looking around for land elsewhere, to be used for such purposes as dumping convicts. In 1788 the first colonists settled in a place they called Sydney.

At that time perhaps half a million or possibly a million people lived in Australia. They are usually called Aborigines, which just means "original inhabitants." Their ancestors arrived in the continent around 50,000 years ago. When the Europeans arrived the number of languages was around 270, which means that one or two thousand people spoke each language, on average. As has been pointed out before, this kind of situation has been typical for humans during most of the time that the species has existed.

The Europeans regarded the original inhabitants as an inferior race and treated them harshly. Nowadays about 17 million people inhabit Australia, and about 99 per cent speak English. The Aborigines constitute a small minority of a few hundred thousand. Many of their languages are gone. Some are still spoken, but in many communities there are only elderly speakers, as the children tend to shift to English. The final disappearance of these languages seems to be a matter of time.

In this way English has prevailed over a whole continent, granted that it is more impressive in terms of surface than in terms of population. There are considerable English-speaking populations in other parts of the world too. As late as the 1830s British people started to settle in great numbers in New Zealand which was then inhabited only by the Maori, a group of people with a language of its own. Now there are about three and a half million people, of which a quarter million are Maoris. The whole population uses English, and some Maoris also speak Maori.

WHAT HAPPENED?

When the Europeans found their way over the seas to all other countries it spelt the beginning of great reversals also for the languages of the world. Now, after five centuries, it can be seen clearly that the voyages over the seas were the beginning of the end for all very small languages, and the start of the era of big languages.

Before agriculture, up to about 10,000 years ago all people lived in fairly small groups, and few or no languages were spoken by more than a few thousand people. Through a series of events that have been partly traced in this book large languages appeared in conjunction with large political units in parts of Europe, Africa, and Asia. America and Australia did not partake very much in that development. In the last few centuries the Europeans have transferred their agriculture, some of their people, and a few of their languages to those parts of the world. The original small languages have disappeared or are disappearing, and a few European languages have become extremely large, in terms of numbers of speakers.

In the last five centuries there has been an accelerating growth of the world population. This is important in several ways. It means, among other things, that practically all languages have gained speakers. The exceptions are mainly small languages used by communities of gatherers and hunters. However, the population growth did not in itself change the proportions between the languages; that was effected by the invasions. Half a millennium ago there were around 70 million people in Europe, and about thirty major languages. Now there are 700 million people, but the major languages are about as many as before; actually, they are mainly the same ones. On the American continent the population has grown at a similar rate, from about 50 million to around 700 million. But there were 1,000 languages or more 500 years ago, and there are three very large ones now.

Still there are some areas in the world with very many languages. They represent a state that was universal for a very long time. Many of the small languages of Asia, Europe, and northern Africa gave way to larger languages with hundreds of thousands or even a few million speakers. Languages with very many speakers, 100 million or more, are a comparatively recent phenomenon. Chinese reached that level several hundred years ago. The other ones that have attained it are some Asian languages of densely populated areas, such as Hindi, Bengali, and Japanese, the previously very expansive Arabic and the more recently expansive languages English, Spanish, Portuguese ,and Russian.

The main trend, then, during the last millennium has been that a few languages have become very large, while many small ones have disappeared. This trend continues, and we will return to it. However, first a chapter about how new languages have been created even in the last few centuries.

Chapter 10

How Languages Are Born —or Made

This chapter provides a number of examples of how new languages have come into being in the last 400 years. They are from various parts of the world: the West Indies, southern Africa, and Norway. Also, the reasons why the new languages appeared are quite different. However, there are some interesting similarities that will be summed up at the end of the chapter.

SLAVE TRADE, LANGUAGE MUTILATION, AND LANGUAGE BIRTH

The Europeans travelled over the seas in order to enrich themselves, and many attained their goal. Much of what they did was sheer robbery, but in the long run business and production are safer ways to make fortunes. The original enticement was the spice trade with the Far East, and other activities were soon added.

A very important one was to run plantations in newly conquered territories. Europe was to be provided with sugar, cotton, and other products that could be grown in a tropical climate. Plantations were created in the islands of the West Indies, in the American mainland from southern North America to northeastern South America, in islands and coastal strips of the Indian Ocean, and also farther eastwards.

Plantations were labour intensive, and the Europeans themselves did not do the manual work. They needed many labourers, who usually could not be found where the plantations were located. The West Indies was sparsely populated before the European invasion, and that population was almost extinguished during the first century of European rule.

The solution was to buy slaves on a large scale. Slavery was by no means a novelty; it was practised in many parts of the world. In Europe, however, outright slavery and slave trade had ceased to exist during the Middle Ages. When the plantations began to operate and turned out to be very profitable, demand for labour grew rapidly, and the Europeans started buying slaves in West Africa for exportation westwards.

This was one leg in a very lucrative transatlantic trade. The ships left the harbours of western Europe loaded with cloth, glassware, and other products that were in demand in West Africa. The load was sold there; slaves were bought and taken to the West Indies. From there, the ships sailed back to Europe with sugar or cotton. The profit on a trip of this kind could be extremely high.

For the slaves, the operation had no advantages. They were people who had had the misfortune of being caught, often by an expedition from some neighbouring state. In West Africa there are very many small languages, and there were many small, competing states. In the era of slave trade some of these states were in the business of capturing people from other states in order to sell them.

The slaves were crammed into the ships and were freighted in the cheapest possible way, like a livestock transport. Mortality on the ships was very high. The ones who survived were put into hard, life-long labour on a plantation that was usually located in an isolated area, without many contacts with the outside world.

Initially, the slaves naturally spoke their own languages. But there were rarely more than a few in a plantation who had the same mother tongue. In order to minimize the considerable risks of mutiny and organized escape the slave traders often tried to mix different groups as much as possible in the slave depots along the west coast of Africa, and the buyers applied the same strategy again. The idea was to make communication among the slaves difficult, and as so many languages are spoken in West Africa, this often had the intended effect.

New slaves on a plantation therefore had no common language. On the other hand, they had to learn some of the slave-drivers' language, as it was used for orders and other elementary communication. As a result, the first generation of slaves were deprived of the use of their native language but were not admitted into a new language community. They lost their linguistic as well as their social identity.

However, no human beings can be completely without a language, and in the plantations new languages emerged in unusual ways. Exactly what happened is not easy to say, as there are few detailed descriptions from plantations in the early period. That is not surprising. The only people who could have made written accounts were the plantation owners and the ones in their immediate environment, and they had reasons not to divulge what was going on.

There is fair agreement that what was used in the earliest period was a pidgin language. Pidgin languages are found not only in connection with the slave trade but have existed and exist in several parts of the world. Sometimes people without any language in common still need to communicate, for example in order to trade with each other or to exchange commands and questions in a workplace. They first learn single words from each other. Fairly soon, a number of words and phrases become the common property of the group, and if the contacts prevail for a number of years a restricted language may emerge, with a small vocabulary and some grammatical rules, but usually quite variable from speaker to speaker. Such a language is a pidgin language. Often it exists for only a short time, but under appropriate circumstances it may survive for centuries, for example when people from many linguistic groups meet regularly at marketplaces.

The pidgin languages in the plantations naturally imported most of the words from the language of the slave-drivers. That was usually English or French, as Britain and France were the most active nations in the plantation business during the heyday of the slave trade in the seventeenth and eighteenth centuries. Thus the new slaves communicated with the slave owners and partly among themselves in a very restricted language consisting mostly of English or French words and with a grammar that was simple but not necessarily very similar to that of English or French.

Then the next generation came along. There were slaves of both sexes, and their children naturally grew up among the slaves. Within the families the parents did not necessarily speak any common language, and in the community at large the pidgin language was what existed. But a pidgin language is not a complete language. The children needed a full language and created it for themselves, departing from the pidgin language. In that way the Creole languages were formed.

At least that is what many people think. There are also other ideas concerning their emergence, but first it may be a good idea to present a sample of such a language. One of the Creole languages based on English is spoken on the island of Nevis in the Caribbean. The text below is written in that language, which usually does not appear in writing. It is a rendering of spoken language, originally published in a newspaper.

Wen ting waantin a Niivis, dem tap lang fu du, an wen dem du, dem tap langa fu don.—Mi hia piipl a aks if mi an yu no wiari chat. Taal! Bikaas aabi a get wondaful rizol.

In standard English this means:

When something is needed in Nevis, they take a long time to do it, and when they do it, they take longer to get it done.—I hear people asking if I and you aren't weary of talking. Not at all! Because we are getting wonderful results.

Most of the words in the text from Nevis are recognizable as English ones, and often the difference is merely a matter of spelling. Sometimes groups of consonants are simplified, as in *an* for English "and." But some words are different, such as *tap* for "take" and *aabi* for "we."

The grammar is not very similar to that of English. For example, clauses with an adjective do not need an inflected verb: *mi an yu no wiari* means "I and you are not weary." Nouns do not necessarily take a plural *–s*: *rizol* means "results." The verbs have no special forms for past tense. On the other hand, there are markers in front of verbs. In the text there are the phrases *piipl a aks* for "people are asking" and *aabi a get* for "we are getting." The marker *a* clearly means about the same as "are" (or some other form of "be") before the verb, and "-ing" after it; that is what is called the progressive form in standard English.

There are other markers of a similar kind in the language. *Piipl bin aks* means "people asked." Thus the marker *bin* (which originally comes from the English form "been") has the meaning of past tense. It is also possible to combine the markers: *piipl bin a aks* means "people were asking." Someone who knows just the meaning of the stems in English cannot possibly understand such expressions. The Creole language has a grammar of its own.

ARE CREOLE LANGUAGES LANGUAGES?

As has been seen, a Creole language is not very similar to the European language it has taken most of its words from. A person who knows only standard English does not understand the language of Nevis, and vice versa. Is it a language of its own? The answers have varied.

The Creole languages emerged mainly in the seventeenth and eighteenth centuries, and many of them are still spoken. For a long time, at least up to the end of the nineteenth century, no one who was not a speaker of a Creole language believed that they were anything else than bad English (or French, or Portuguese, etc.). Around that time a few linguists started to take an interest in these forms of speech, but systematic research did not really begin until the 1960s. Those linguists who work with description and analysis regard them as separate languages, not as forms of the European language.

The main reason is a purely linguistic one. If two forms of speech show fundamental differences in the way they denote major linguistic categories such as tense and number, the linguistic systems are very dissimilar from a linguist's point of view, even if the vocabularies are partly identical.

However, it has been proposed earlier in this book that whether a form of speech is a language of its own has to be decided by the speakers themselves. It is what they say and think about their way of speech that decides what it actually is. Often this is a question of names, for a language needs a name in order to be considered to exist. A name often does not appear until the language acquires a written form, as we have seen.

The language forms that modern researchers have identified as Creole languages are around fifty altogether. Each of them has a vocabulary based upon one of English, French, Portuguese, Spanish, or Dutch. Most of them are used by fairly few people, from a few hundred up to a few hundred thousand.

In most cases we cannot be too sure about what the speakers themselves think of their form of speech, as this has by no means always been recorded by researchers. Some are obviously languages in their own right, in the view of speakers and others alike. The clearest case is Haitian, which is spoken as a native language by almost all the 6 million citizens of Haiti. It has a name of its own, there is an official orthography as well as literary works, and the language is used for instruction in elementary school. Haitian has taken its vocabulary from French, but only a small élite in Haiti uses standard French, and contacts between the two languages are comparatively insignificant; Haitian is developing in a direction of its own. Another well-established Creole language is Papiamentu, used by a few hundred thousand people on Curaçao and neighbouring islands outside Venezuela. As a consequence of history its vocabulary stems from three European languages: Spanish, Portuguese, and Dutch.

In many cases, however, the situation is quite different. Most of these speech forms are designated by such terms as "Barbadian Creole English" or "Lesser Antillean French Creole." These names are clearly not used by the speakers but are scholarly classifications. The speakers themselves do not necessarily employ any particular name for what they speak. From several places there is evidence that they use such expressions as *lingo* or *patois*. That is, they talk about their "idiom" or "dialect" or something similar, without using any other label. Also, it is not unusual for speakers to insist that what they speak is a form of English, or French, etc.

This is to say that these forms are actually not languages in the sense that the speakers themselves think that they are independent linguistic units. The reason for this is just what one might expect. Speakers of Creole languages are to a considerable extent descendants of slaves, and they have often inherited their low status and vulnerable position. They mostly do not take pride in their language, but regard it as an inferior variant of something else that has higher rank and prestige. Often they are ashamed of speaking Creole. Neither the speakers nor their languages enjoy esteem in the societies where they live, for mostly Creole speakers do not constitute the majority, as they happen to do in Haiti and Curaçao, but are disadvantaged minorities, and their language forms often compete with the standard language, English or French. It is also inappropriate to draw an absolute demarcation line between the standard language and the Creole, as there may be many intermediate forms.

In sum, then, a few Creoles are unquestionably languages of their own, but many others are regarded as separate languages mainly by linguists, while the speakers see the matter differently. The view proposed here is that in such situations the speakers have the last word, as the language form belongs to them.

THE REMARKABLE SIMILARITIES

All students of Creole languages are intrigued and fascinated by a remarkable fact: they are all similar. Not in the way that one would expect, that their grammars are like those of the European languages, but quite the opposite. They all have grammars that resemble each other but are very unlike the European ones. Their words may come from English or from Portuguese, and they may be found in the Caribbean or on an island in the Indian Ocean, at the opposite side of the globe; the similarities are there all the same.

One of these resemblances is found in the verbal systems. Markers such as the ones we described above are found in almost all Creole languages, and they work more or less in the same way in all the languages. For example, the Creoles with a French vocabulary often have a marker *pe* (from French *après*) with the same meaning and the same use as *a* in Nevis Creole. Sometimes the form of the marker is *ap* (also from *après*), but that makes no change to the meaning.

There are several such grammatical similarities between all or most Creole languages. How can this be? They emerged at different places and at different times, and in several cases there cannot have been any direct contact at all. The problem has given rise to a whole literature and many learned disputes. A number of theories have been proposed.

The most spectacular one is that the grammar of Creole languages is the grammar that emerges when children have to form a language of their own, without good models from the adults. Those grammatical systems would then be instances of a kind of universal grammar supposed to be innate in human beings and available in the absence of external models. A somewhat similar but less sensational idea is that the grammar of Creole languages is the type of grammar that humans can most easily understand and learn.

A completely different kind of explanation is that all Creole languages are descendants of one original pidgin language used by the Portuguese. There probably existed a widespread pidgin based on Portuguese, and it seems to have left traces in most pidgins and Creoles. For example, they almost always include the word *pikin* or *pikanin*, "small," which stems from Portuguese *pequeno* or Spanish *pequeño* or *pequeñín*.

A third way to account for the similarities is to look for

models in the West African languages that were the native tongues of many of the slaves.

A fourth attempt is to point out that for many of the peculiarities of Creole languages there seem to exist forerunners in the European languages, or in some of their dialects. What has been going on, then, would have been ordinary linguistic change, albeit at an accelerated speed. The Creole languages would be harbingers of the future shape of English or French. Certain French researchers have even launched the term *français avancé*, "advanced French," to denote the French-based Creole languages.

All those attempts at an explanation suffer from the weakness that they can account for some of the similarities but not for others. There are also some striking parallels that have still other reasons. For example, the text above contains the word *aks* for "ask," and this word appears in many English-based Creoles. However, it is not an innovation at all in these languages, but a dialectal variant of the English word. The first attested example is more than a thousand years old. Some of the slave-drivers have left a trace of their native dialect.

So some of the similarities turn out to have fairly trivial causes. Still, some of the parallels in grammar are very striking but can hardly have had a common origin. This means that similar grammatical devices, such as the particles corresponding to progressive form in English, must have been invented several times in different places. This must mean that those devices somehow were near at hand for the creators of the new languages.

However, the idea that this represents an innate universal grammar is not the only possible way to account for it. After all, those grammatical devices are not particularly frequent in other languages of the world. They ought to be so, if humans were genetically predisposed to use them. It is just as possible that these devices are the ones that come most naturally to people who have some knowledge both of a west European language and of one or several West African languages. If that is so, which I suspect, the problem is still very interesting, but it may not be very relevant for the study of our innate linguistic capacity.

But that is just my personal opinion, and most researchers in the field may opt for other ideas. No final solution to the problem of the similarities between Creoles seems to be in sight.

CREOLE LANGUAGES AND LANGUAGE CHANGE

An important lesson from the Creole languages is that new language forms can emerge very rapidly in certain circumstances. If the situation demands a new language, a new language will be created. Humans possess enormous linguistic creativity that can be used to construct something entirely novel, if that is necessary.

One may ask why the slaves did this, rather than simply learning the language of the slave-drivers, English or French. There is an answer that was stated openly a couple of generations ago and still lies hidden behind some of the discussions about Creole languages: that the slaves were too stupid to learn these languages well. This is one of the reasons why Creole languages are often looked down upon, and why many speakers are ashamed of their languages.

Now, there are actually no indications that Africans are less intelligent or less capable of learning languages than other people (even if racist myths are still circulating). Also, millions of Africans today speak perfect English, French, or Portuguese. The reason why the slaves created their own language forms was certainly another one.

It was a question of linguistic identity. All human beings have a basic need for a first language that is used in the family and with the most intimate friends and is an important part of one's person. Some people have two (or even more) such languages, but all need at least one. When the slaves were transported from Africa the languages were taken from them. They were isolated and put under masters who were alien and detestable. To create an identity of one's own within the language of such masters was impossible as well as repugnant. Rather, the slaves invented a linguistic space for themselves, where they could at least feel that their language belonged to them.

In this way, the American continent and its islands acquired a number of new languages for the outcasts in addition to the three large European languages for the great majority of ordinary members of society. This shows, among other things, that history does not incessantly move in the same direction, towards larger and more stable languages. Small, isolated societies such as the plantations may give birth to small, isolated languages in a short time.

AFRIKAANS—GERMANIC AND AFRICAN

In 1652, when European ships had already sailed along the coasts of Africa for a century and a half, the Dutch East India Company decided to procure a base near the Cape of Good Hope, at the southernmost tip of the continent. A small group of Dutchmen under Jan van Riebeeck set up a station by the shore at the foot of Table Mountain, just where the centre of Cape Town is still located.

The colony grew very slowly, mostly through accretion from the Khoi people who were the original inhabitants, and through immigration of Europeans of several nationalities. There was also a group of people from Dutch India (present-day Indonesia). Not many came from the Netherlands. After a little more than 150 years, in 1806, Britain took control of the colony. At that time the colony comprised about 15,000 people.

As early as that, there are some notes about the language. What was spoken was not exactly the kind of Dutch one could hear in Amsterdam but something rather far removed from that. The descriptions are not flattering; it was perceived as a strange jargon.

The language of Cape Town remained and spread over a large area with great speed. British rule became very unpopular among the original colonists who were mainly farmers, or *boere* in their own language; in English they were soon called Boers. They particularly disliked the fact that the British abolished slavery in the 1830s, as their economy was largely based upon slave labour. Many Boers left the British colony in their oxcarts to seek new land in the north and north-east. Through this migration, called *die grote trek* or "the Great Trek," the Boers dispersed over the better part of what is now South Africa.

In the 1850s the Boers founded two independent states northeast of the Cape colony, The Orange Free State and Transvaal. After several difficulties and a great war between the Boers and the British, the Union of South Africa was formed in 1910; it included both the Cape Province and the Boer states. The English and the Boers shared the political power, while the majority was not granted any influence.

The Boers who lived in the Cape colony around 1800 spoke a language that did not quite sound like Dutch. Still, they did consider it to be a form of the Dutch language, and the written language was the same as in the Netherlands.

However, after the middle of the nineteenth century, when the Boer republics had been created, there ensued a discussion about the language. At that time some texts had already been published that approached the spoken language. Around the beginning of the 1870s a group of strongly nationalistic Boers started discussing the possibility of a new written language. It seems that it was suggested at that time that the name of the language should be *Afrikaans*; the Boers name themselves *Afrikaners* in their own language.

For some time this proposal seemed to be forgotten, something that is clearly connected with the fact that the Boer republics were in considerable trouble. But after the Boer War the idea surfaced once more, and gained enormous momentum. From around 1905 there was intensive work with strong political backing. An orthography was adopted, journals and books were published, a translation of the Bible was started, to be completed in 1933, and textbooks, grammars, and dictionaries were composed. The language soon became a medium of instruction and a major subject in schools. Within a few decades Afrikaans was firmly established as an official language alongside English in the Union of South Africa.

In the course of the twentieth century Afrikaans has also become an important literary language, with authors such as Breyten Breytenbach and André Brink. About 5 million people out of the 42 million in South Africa speak it and it is one of the official languages, which are now eleven.

Thus Afrikaans became a language about a century ago. It is obvious that it was born for political and national reasons. The Boers no longer had important political and cultural ties with the Netherlands; actually, those ties had been fairly weak for centuries. They were building their own states, in which they constituted a ruling minority in the midst of a majority of people speaking other languages. They competed with the English. For all these reasons they were in great need of a national identity of their own, and the language they created for themselves contributed to it.

AFRIKAANS—DIALECT OR CREOLE LANGUAGE?

Dutch and Afrikaans resemble each other a great deal, but the differences are large enough for them not to be mutually intelligible, at least not without some training. Some differences, particularly those in vocabulary, are caused by the simple fact that the languages have not been in contact for a long time. Other differences may have to do with old dialectal variation, as van Riebeeck and many of his companions spoke a southern dialect of Dutch, while the modern standard Dutch language is mainly based on northern dialects.

There are however more basic discrepancies. The most important one concerns the verbs. In Afrikaans, verbs are almost not at all inflected for person; the old Germanic endings have disappeared even more thoroughly than in English, which retains −s in the third person plural and several forms for the verb "to be." In Dutch, however, the verbal inflection is kept. Compare the forms for the verb "to be" in the present tense in Table 10.1:

TABLE 10.1. *The verb "to be" in English,*
Dutch, and Afrikaans

English	Dutch	Afrikaans
I am	ik ben	ek is
you are	jij bent	tjy is
he is	hij is	hy is
we are	wij zijn	ons is
you are	jullie zijn	julle is
they are	zij zijn	hulle is

Afrikaans has simplified the verbal system in another respect too. Dutch has three forms that refer to the past, just like English; they are usually called past, perfect, and pluperfect tense, as in English *I called, I have called, I had called.* In Dutch, these three forms would be *ik riep, ik heb geroepen, ik had geroepen.* But in Afrikaans there is just one form, *ek het geroep.* It is used in all cases when one of the three forms is employed in Dutch or English.

There are also differences in syntax. For example, Afrikaans uses a double negation in many cases, as in *ek sal nie praat nie,* literally "I shall not talk not."

Altogether, the changes that Afrikaans has undergone are more radical than one would easily expect in an isolated dialect of a language, and partly they seem to be of a different nature. Most of the changes also occurred in a short time-span, from 1652 to around 1800, when the language seems already to have been quite similar to the modern one.

This has led to a number of speculations. As early as 100 years ago one researcher suggested that this language is partly similar to the Creole languages that were discussed above. He thought the reason for this Creolization might have been the mixing of languages in the early times of the colony, when there were many speakers of Khoi languages and also a number of slaves from Dutch India. Those latter people used a form of Portuguese, or a Portuguese-based Creole, as their common language. The South African establishment has vehemently opposed hypotheses of this kind. Their preferred alternative explanation is that Afrikaans is the way it is because van Riebeeck and his followers spoke that way.

Probably there is some truth in the arguments of both sides. In any case, it is quite interesting that a language can change in several important respects in just a few generations, although the social situation clearly was not nearly as catastrophic as it was in the slave plantations where the Creole languages were born. In certain circumstances language forms may be very prone to change.

This does not mean, however, that they thereby acquire the status of languages of their own. The language of the Cape colony was still Dutch at the beginning of the nineteenth century, in spite of the fact that all the important changes had already taken place. It became a language of its own when its speakers became rulers in a new state 100 years later. Language change is one thing, and change in the status of a language is something entirely different.

NORWEGIAN—ONE LANGUAGE OR TWO?

The Scandinavian languages, which are spoken in Sweden, Denmark, Norway, Iceland, and the Faeroes, have a common origin. Runes were used from a very early time, and a written language with Latin letters was also developed, first in Iceland. There were dialectal differences, of course, and in the thirteenth and fourteenth centuries three distinct written languages were developed, one each for the kingdoms of Denmark, Norway, and Sweden.

However, only two of these remained in use. The Swedish and Danish written languages were closely associated with their respective states, and they are still official and dominating languages in Sweden and Denmark, respectively. The Norwegian language did not receive the same political support, as the kings of Norway gradually lost their power and influence. During most of the fourteenth century there was a union of Sweden and Norway, and from the end of that century the union comprised all three countries, with a succession of Danish kings. Sweden left the union after some time, finally in 1521, but Norway in practice became a part of Denmark. The separate written language gave way to the Danish one. When the countries became Protestant in the early sixteenth century the Latin Bible was exchanged for one in Danish; no translation into Norwegian was made. From that time and onwards for 300 years, Danish was the written language of Norway.

The spoken language was a different matter. Along the fjords and in the mountain valleys, Norwegian dialects developed in their own way, with very little influence from Danish. In the towns, the written language was fairly important, and those who obtained higher education did so in Denmark or in schools where Danish was used and taught. There developed a spoken language with much Danish vocabulary and some Danish morphology.

In the Napoleonic wars the Danes were in the wrong alliance, and as a consequence they lost Norway. From 1814 the country was ruled by the king of Sweden, but attained a fairly autonomous position. It grew more independent, and when the union with Sweden was dissolved in 1905 that was an inevitable consequence of the fact that the Norwegians had a fully functioning state, a strong feeling of national identity, and not least a new Norwegian language. Or possibly two.

A few decades after the liberation from Denmark Norwegian writers started to introduce Norwegian words and phrases in the written language in a conscious way. An early example is provided by a famous collection of folk tales, *Norske folkeventyr*, published in the 1840s. Later authors added more Norwegian elements, so that the result was a much modified written language, often called Danish-Norwegian, *dansk-norsk*. Several great Norwegian writers, including Ibsen, used this language.

So the Danish written language gradually became more similar to spoken urban Norwegian. This was done quite deliberately. An eminent linguist, Knud Knudsen, was one of the ideologues of this development. He and his followers strived to create a Norwegian written language in the reformist way, through gradual changes of the Danish one.

There was also a competing, more revolutionary movement. Its goal was to create an entirely new Norwegian written language, based upon Norwegian rural dialects and to some extent on the medieval Norwegian written language. The initiator was Ivar Aasen, who studied rural dialects thoroughly and created a written language largely based on them. He called it *landsmål*, "country language." He wrote literary works himself in this language, and others followed suite.

In this way two written languages emerged in Norway within half a century after the disappearance of the Danish influence. Both received strong support, but from different quarters. Danish-Norwegian was strong in the urban areas, particularly so in the capital Christiania (later Oslo), and in the surrounding south-eastern part of the country. *Landsmål* was favoured in the rural areas, especially in the western districts. Neither prevailed; both were recognized as official written languages. More than a century ago, in an edict of 1892 concerning elementary school, it was decreed that the school board could choose which language was to be used actively in the school but that all children had to learn to read both. This has not changed, in principle. However, both written forms are now known by different names. What was called Danish-Norwegian in the nineteenth century is now officially called *bokmål*, "book language," and the language dubbed *landsmål* by Aasen is nowadays called *nynorsk*, "new Norwegian."

For long periods there have been acrimonious battles between the adherents of these two forms. There are political undercurrents in these fights. New Norwegian is connected with radical political views, but also with nationalism and with rural society, while *bokmål* associates with conservatism and with urban élites.

However, the situation now is much calmer than it used to be. The two written language forms coexist fairly peacefully. The boundaries also are becoming somewhat blurred. Writers do not necessarily feel that they have to stick faithfully to one norm or the other, so there is much room for individual variation.

Norwegian is an unusual case. It is true that there are many states that have created and upheld a separate written language for political and national reasons. Afrikaans is a good example. There is also nothing strange in the fact that several alternative variants were proposed. What is extremely remarkable is that the new state sanctioned two different written languages. The only similar case I know of is that of the two written versions of Modern Greek, *kathareuousa* and *dimotiki*: this was discussed in the chapter on Greek above. But there, the state has always been in favour of one or the other, depending on the political situation.

The Norwegian way of allowing both written languages with equal rights may seem quite dangerous, for it might have meant a split into two languages, two nationalities, and two states.

This did not happen, and there is an obvious reason. In spite of the fact that the proponents of the two forms differed in their views on language and also on politics and other matters they agreed completely on a more fundamental matter. They all thought, and think, that there is one Norway and one Norwegian language. Nation-building always ranked above the language question. Because of that it was politically possible to allow both language forms.

For that reason it also seems incorrect to maintain that Norway really has two written languages. Again, the existence of languages is a matter that is determined by the users. If Norwegians had believed that the two forms represent independent languages, that would have been decisive. But according to law and usage they are just two ways of representing the same spoken language in written form. Norway seems to have one language with two written norms. This is very unusual, but obviously not impossible.

HOW SPOKEN LANGUAGE BECOMES WRITTEN LANGUAGE—OR VICE VERSA

In southern Africa the Sotho languages are spoken over a vast area, including large parts of northern South Africa, the whole of Lesotho, and the whole of Botswana.

Sotho is a group of languages within the larger Bantu group. The language forms within the Sotho group do not differ very much; people from different parts of this large region can understand each other without major problems.

Do people speak one language or several related languages in the Sotho area? As has been pointed out a few times already, the answer hinges on what the speakers themselves think. This has changed fairly recently, in connection with social and political changes.

Before the European intrusion in the nineteenth century, the whole area was organized politically as many small, independent states. The number of citizens in a state could vary from a few thousand to perhaps two hundred thousand. The number of states may have been a hundred, or possibly more. The structure was not very stable; states fairly often split and sometimes amalgamated.

As was natural, each state had a name. The name was used primarily for the citizens, not for the area where they lived. Just like other nouns in Bantu languages, names are inflected through prefixes that are added to the stem. A member of the Kwena state was called a *Mokwena*; two or more were *Bakwena*. In the same way, a member of the Tlhaping state was a *Motlhaping*, in the plural *Batlhaping*.

For each name, it is also possible to form an abstract noun by adding the prefix *se-*. For the two examples given, that produces *Sekwena* and *Setlhaping*. The noun *Sekwena* means approximately "that which is Kwena," that is "customs and habits among the Kwena," or more restrictedly "the language spoken by the Kwena."

So, it is possible to make a language name out of any name of a state. This is partly similar to formations like Russian from Russia and Persian from Persia in English. But these African states were quite small and had very similar spoken languages, so from a linguistic point of view it is more like using separate words for "the Cambridge dialect," "the Brighton dialect," and so on. There is one crucial difference, though. In this area there was probably no common name for all the speech forms, such as "English" for all English dialects. The concept of Sotho languages has been introduced by linguists and the name has been taken arbitrarily from one of the largest languages, Sesotho, spoken by the Basotho in their state, which is nowadays called Lesotho. In these languages there was just one name for the speech form of each state, and no common name.

If languages are such linguistic units that have independent names of their own there were at least 100 languages in this area at the beginning of the nineteenth century. Also, languages could appear rapidly, and likewise disappear. When the Ngwato state was created through secession from the Kwena state, it immediately became possible to talk about the new language *Sengwato*. Although this may seem disconcerting to modern Europeans it does not seem that it created any problems for the people involved.

The first steps towards change were taken by Europeans. The Scottish missionary Robert Moffat arrived to Kuruman in the south-western part of the area in the 1820s. He immediately started translating the Bible into the language spoken at that place and printed the Gospel of Luke as early as 1826. Eventually he translated the whole Bible as well as a number of other works, mainly of a religious nature. The language into which he translated was called by him "Sechuana" (the modern spelling is "Setswana"); it is not the name of a state and may possibly have been the common name for a larger unit. Through the translations a first written language came into being in this area, and it was connected with a language name.

About a decade later than Moffat, a group of French Protestant missionaries came to the south-eastern part of the area, to the Sotho state. Their leader Eugène Casalis knew about Moffat and his work, but still decided to make a separate translation of the Bible. Of course he used the language form current among the Basotho, which was in some respects different from that which Moffat had learnt. Eventually the French too completed a translation of the whole Bible.

It is very interesting to note what names Casalis employs for the language. In the first publications he calls it *séchuana* in French, implying that he translates into the same language as Moffat. After a number of years, however, he and his group start using the name *sésotho*, which of course was the name the Basotho themselves used for their language. A reasonable explanation for their change may be that those missionaries, who had invested a large amount of work in a new translation of the Bible, preferred to see it as a rendering in a completely new language rather than a new translation into the language Moffat had already provided with a Bible. In this way a second written language, Sesotho, was established.

A few decades later history repeated itself. In the 1870s German missionaries started a mission in the Pedi state in the north-western part of the area. They decided to produce a Bible translation of their own into the language form they encountered in that area. At first they employed the language name of Sesotho, or Sotho, just like the French missionaries. Later on, however, they changed their mind and decided that the language they wrote should be called either Northern Sotho or Pedi (or Sepedi).

At the end of the nineteenth century, then, there were three written languages: Setswana, Sesotho, and Sepedi. Each one was introduced by one group of missionaries, and there were a few printed texts in each language, mainly religious ones but also some schoolbooks, including orthographies, grammars, and dictionaries for the languages.

These written languages were of limited significance at this time, for the missionaries had moderate success and only a small proportion of the children attended the mission schools. People in general probably still used just the traditional language names such as Sekwena, Setlhaping, and so on, for the languages they spoke.

Times changed, however. There arrived not only more missionaries but also the Boers in their *trek* from the Cape colony, then the English military forces and after them the colonial administrators. The 100 independent states became parts of three political entities. Most of the area was included in the Union of South Africa. A vast but very sparsely populated region in the north became the British protectorate of Bechuanaland, and the Sotho state, located in a mountain range in the midst of South Africa, was transformed into the protectorate of Basutoland.

In the first half of the twentieth century, non-confessional schools and boards of education made their appearance both in South Africa and in the British protectorates. Where there are schools with elementary instruction in reading and writing, there also must be orthographies and other established language norms. On the whole, the educational authorities took over the three written languages elaborated by the missionaries and put them into use in three different parts of the area. In this way the children who went to school learnt to write one of the languages Setswana, Sesotho, or Sepedi, and nothing else. Setswana (also called Tswana) was used in Bechuanaland and South Africa, Sesotho (Sotho) in Basutoland and South Africa, and Sepedi (Pedi)/Northern Sotho only in northernmost South Africa.

In the 1960s, the Protectorates were liberated from Britain and became the independent states Botswana and Lesotho. By this time it was quite clear at least to the leaders that there was one language in each state, Setswana and Sesotho respectively. Since then, things have moved fast.

In Botswana now a solid majority of children pass through nine years of school and learn to read and write in Setswana as a matter of course. The language is much used in the media and in official contexts, in competition with English. The formula recognized by government is that English is the official language, and Setswana is the national one.

There is a definite change in the use of language names. Only four or five decades ago the names of the traditional small units were in general use: a person who was a Mokwena considered herself or himself to speak Sekwena. Nowadays all except perhaps some very old people are of the opinion that the language they speak is Setswana.

At the same time, a new standard for the spoken language is developing. A generation ago all people spoke their home dialect as a matter of course and did not think of any other way of speaking as being better or more prestigious. Nowadays many people clearly strive to talk a standard language, close to the norm for the written language. This written norm is of course the one stipulated by the school authorities.

HOW LANGUAGES COME INTO BEING

A number of examples of how languages have come into being during the last centuries have been presented in this chapter.

They differ in several respects, but one may draw some conclusions about what is necessary for the birth of a new language.

In the first place there is a purely linguistic prerequisite. The language has to have a name. A language without a name does not exist, for the simple reason that it is not possible to talk about it. The name may come into being in various ways, either through invention or through redefinition of a name that existed before. Anyhow, it seems to be a rule without exception in our time that the language name appears when the language is first used as a written language, or soon after that. It is the written language that is perceived as existing in its own right.

Secondly, a language is much helped if it has a political base. Haitian and Afrikaans, Norwegian and Setswana have very different histories, but they are all main languages in independent states. In two of the cases, Norwegian and Afrikaans, it is obvious that the emerging states needed languages of their own to strengthen national identity. However, this kind of backing is not an absolute requirement. Sepedi emerged around the same time as Setswana and in approximately the same way, although it did not have the support of an independent state, and there are several such examples. The languages that dominate a nation state are in a much better position than the others, though.

Thirdly, it does not matter much how similar the language is to other languages. Language change does not in itself necessarily create new languages, as was seen in the case of Creole languages. Several of these are not regarded as languages of their own by anyone except a small number of linguists, in spite of the fact that they may be quite dissimilar to other language forms. On the other hand, Norwegian is close to both Danish and

Swedish, and did not change very dramatically in the nineteenth century. What happened was mostly a change in the politics of language, not a language change.

In sum, quite a few things can be said about how languages are born. The next chapter is about something that is much more common in our time, how languages cease to exist.

Chapter 11
How Languages Disappear

For a long time the language of Scotland was Gaelic, a Celtic language. In the last few centuries Gaelic has retreated, and English has become dominating. In most parts of Scotland Gaelic has disappeared completely. What happened to the dialect of Gaelic spoken in East Sutherland is particularly well documented.

Up to the eighteenth century almost the entire population spoke Gaelic. Their livelihood was farming on the fairly meagre land that they held as tenants of the landowner, Lady Sutherland. But as the demand for wool and mutton was large and growing, this landowner, like others, decided to end the leases to crop farmers and use the land for sheep instead. Most of the tenants were just thrown out of their farms. One of the reasons for the total disregard of these people seems to have been the fact that they did not speak English. Patrick Sellar, Lady Sutherland's factor who was directly responsible for the evictions, wrote about "their obstinate adherence to the barbarous jargon of the times when Europe was possessed by Savages." English-speaking people from the lowlands were recruited as sheep-farmers. The former tenants were given an opportunity to settle along the shore, as it was assumed that they might make a living by fishing.

This policy succeeded in the sense that their descendants are still largely fishermen in the coastal villages. However, they became poor and marginalized and have remained so. To begin with they had few contacts with the English-speaking population around them.

In the nineteenth century the English language started to penetrate these villages. The language of the Church was English. When schools started their language was English only. Health care, business, transport, and other contacts with the world outside the villages required knowledge of English.

From the beginning of the twentieth century almost everyone was bilingual, mostly with Gaelic as the first language and English as the second one. But some English-speaking people also moved into the villages, and as they rarely learned Gaelic the spoken language became English whenever an English-speaking person was present. In particular, children with one English-speaking and one Gaelic-speaking parent always heard English at home, and consequently English became their first language.

In this way the language shifted from almost only Gaelic to almost only English in the course of a few generations. The last people who learned Gaelic as a first language from their parents are now very old. The younger ones who know something of the language have learnt it from their grandparents, often quite imperfectly. They are not able to teach their children or grandchildren any more than a few words of the old language. Within a few decades it will have vanished completely as a spoken language (if there is not some miraculous revival). In written form, this particular dialect is attested only through the transcriptions of linguists.

So, around two and a half centuries elapsed from the time when the language was completely dominant to the time when it is just about to disappear completely. First, the speakers were evicted from the country they inhabited in favour of speakers of a politically dominant language. This language then exerted a permanent and gradually growing influence and gained one function in society after another: Church, school, business, and so on. The decisive stage was when children ceased learning the old language as their first language. After that, it has declined very rapidly.

An American researcher, Nancy Dorian, followed the development in East Sutherland in detail for several decades. Among other things, she demonstrated that the language changed fast in the last generations, and not primarily through direct influence from English as one would have thought. Rather, it seems that "ordinary" language change accelerates within a language that has very few speakers.

The excellent book by Nancy Dorian about Gaelic in East Sutherland is entitled *Language Death*, and that expression has become quite current. For my own part I feel rather hesitant about that term. It describes the process well enough, but it also implies that languages have lives. If they have not, they obviously cannot die. This is a natural analogy with human life, but slightly misleading. People use languages, and as long as a language is in use it exists. When it is not in use any more it ceases to exist. That may be a great loss of knowledge, skills, and culture, but it does not normally mean that any group of people cease to use language, through death or otherwise. Rather, they use another language instead.

It is only in the last few decades that researchers have started investigating systematically and in detail how languages may gradually weaken and finally disappear completely. The phenomenon as such is of course not new, but it is becoming more and more frequent. At this time, languages are disappearing at a faster rate than ever before.

THE LANGUAGES WITHOUT A FUTURE

Five to seven thousand languages are spoken on earth at present, but most are used only by a small number of speakers. There are now around 6 billion people. The sixty largest languages, in terms of numbers of speakers, share more than 4 billion speakers among themselves. That is, about 1 per cent of the languages are used by about 75 per cent of the speakers. The remaining languages all have less than 10 million speakers.

Quite a few of the small languages are losing speakers at a rapid pace and may be extinct soon. An even larger number show signs of weakening and may become seriously threatened later on.

As has been amply demonstrated above, languages are not intrinsically stable. At any given time some languages are emerging, and others are disappearing. What is happening right now, however, is of an order of magnitude beyond anything that has occurred earlier. It was pointed out in the beginning of this book that in the Neolithic period there were probably very many small languages, and almost certainly no large ones. In the last three millennia there has been a steady development towards larger languages, but they have always coexisted with several thousand small ones. Nowadays almost all small languages are subjected to pressure from larger languages, and that pressure is growing steadily. As a result, languages are disappearing fast already. There are several indications that this process is accelerating and that within a few generations there will be many fewer languages than now, in spite of the fact that the number of people on earth will continue to grow.

The small languages have few speakers, by definition, and in most cases those speakers lack economic influence and political clout. For this reason not much is heard about the plight of small languages in most parts of the world. Some linguists are aware of the situation and try to inform the public, but in general this important process is going on practically unnoticed.

THE REALIGNMENT OF DIALECTS

What disappeared in East Sutherland was one form of Gaelic, not all Gaelic. It was a form that deviated considerably from other Gaelic, so that it is not obvious whether it was a separate language or a dialect.

In that case, the development was in any case a part of a more general process that leads to loss of a language (or perhaps languages). The speakers shifted to English, not to another form of Gaelic. This was in line with what is going on in other areas of

Scotland, and the eventual result will probably be that all forms of Gaelic are extinguished and English takes over completely.

The loss of dialects in favour of a closely related standard language is another process, which is also quite important at present. Languages with a standard written form and many speakers, like English and French, often comprise a number of quite deviant dialects, particularly in rural areas. Some of these dialects may have developed more or less independently for a very long time. However, for more than a century now the dialects of large European languages have been experiencing considerable influence from the standard languages. Almost all rural dialects tend to lose their locally developed words in favour of items from the standard language. Pronunciation may still be markedly different.

The fact that dialects tend to disappear or at least to become more similar has partly the same causes as the disappearance of languages. Schools, the mass media, and generally improved communications and closer contacts are all in favour of the large standard language. Still, to change a dialect is a much less dramatic shift than to shift to another language, and the effort involved is much smaller.

With these few words we leave the subject of dialects, although they provide a fascinating study. It should be noted, though, that new dialects surface just as old ones fade away. But that could fill another book; the rest of this chapter deals only with radical language shifts.

WHAT WILL BE LEFT?

Will anything remain of the languages that disappear? In most cases very little. Several languages have probably vanished in the last few hundred years without leaving any identifiable traces at all. Nowadays, the languages that go mostly leave a name behind, and fairly often there are some field notes or recordings. If a written text exists it is usually produced by a missionary, perhaps a translation of a gospel and possibly an elementary grammar and a wordlist.

If there is a good description and a reasonable supply of written texts it is possible to learn the language, in principle at least, and even to start speaking it again if anyone is so inclined. The languages that are recorded are thus not irretrievably lost, but are to a certain extent available for the descendants of the speakers, for linguists, and for other interested persons. It is most desirable that all languages that are now seriously endangered should be documented in that way. Unfortunately it does not seem probable that anything like this will happen.

It is of course extremely unusual that a language is actually revived after it has ceased to be spoken. However, there is one well-known instance, which is also a large-scale project. Biblical Hebrew went out of use as a spoken language more than 2,000 years ago, but was taken up again about 100 years ago, and is now both the spoken and the written main language of the new state of Israel. This example shows that it is not correct to regard languages that are not spoken but are attested in writing as "dead." They are not used now, but in principle they may be used again, and the cultural capital represented by the language is not completely gone. It must be realized, though, that a revived language will not be a copy of the original one. Modern Hebrew in Israel has developed into something that is in many respects unlike biblical Hebrew, as is quite natural. A language is a part of the culture in which it is used, and modern Israel is very distant from Israel in biblical times.

Languages without written documentation are definitely lost. What they leave behind may be a number of place-names, perhaps a loanword or two in neighbouring languages, and probably a more or less distinctive accent in the new language among the descendants of the speakers, at least for a few generations. This seems to be the fate in store for very many of the languages spoken today.

HOW LANGUAGES DISAPPEAR

Languages are vanishing in all parts of the world, and the course of events is similar everywhere. People stop using a local language with few speakers and shift to one that has more speakers and is in general use over a larger area. The reasons are similar everywhere. School education is expanding in almost all countries, and is usually offered only in big languages. Business and communications also become more important, which means a larger need for a language used by more people. Health care, paid work, taxes, and social benefits are becoming well known to ever more speakers of small languages. All of these mean more contacts with people who do not belong to the local environment and do not speak the local language.

On top of this, speakers of small languages are often already disadvantaged in terms of land and other resources, as was the case in East Sutherland. They are rarely able to speak to important people in their own language, but have to learn the language of the powerful in order to defend their rights.

Of course there are also differences between countries and between continents. Very broadly speaking, each continent has a situation of its own.

TABLE 11.1. *Geographic distribution of living languages in the year 2000*

	Total Living Languages	%
Africa	2,058	30
Americas	1,013	15
Asia	2,197	32
Europe	230	3
Pacific	1,311	19
Totals	6,809	

Source: B. Grimes, *Ethnologue*, 14th edn. (Dallas: SIL, 2000).

In this context, however, the island of New Guinea has to be counted as a continent, and I will begin with that one. This island has many more languages than any other part of the world. The area is two and a half times that of the British Isles, and the population around 5 million people. The number of languages is estimated at close to 1,000, or something like a fifth of all languages spoken on earth. The island is politically divided: the eastern part is the independent state of Papua New Guinea while the western part is a province of Indonesia and is called Irian Jaya.

Most of New Guinea is hilly and extremely rough country, so that contacts between settlements have been sparse up to a few decades ago. People have lived in small independent groups employing unsophisticated farming, in a type of culture that is often called Upper Neolithic. Almost every village has had and kept its own language. Many of the languages are extremely small, sometimes having less than 100 speakers, and may never have been much larger.

In the twentieth century, and particularly in the last few decades, many villages have got communications, access to schools, regular trade, contacts with missionaries, and much else besides. Those are radical and shocking changes. One consequence of the new era is that the young adults and the children turn from the local languages.

Instead, they take up the language they meet among the people they get in touch with outside the village. It is not one of the world's great languages, but Tok Pisin. This was originally a pidgin language of the type that was discussed above. Its vocabulary comes mainly from English; the name Tok Pisin actually is from English "talk pidgin." It first developed on plantations on the Melanesian islands outside New Guinea, but soon it became a common language of communication in the whole area. It gained a strong foothold in Port Moresby, which became the capital of the new state of Papua New Guinea at independence in 1975. Tok Pisin has become the first language of a fairly large number of people and has acquired an important position as the common means of expression for the new nation.

In Papua New Guinea several hundred languages may be on their way towards extinction right now because of the advancement of Tok Pisin. Unfortunately, the details of this development are not at all well known.

On the southern continent, Australia, the Aborigines were brutally suppressed by the British in the eighteenth and nineteenth centuries. Now, the situation is different. The Aborigines have obtained at last some say of their own, and they are not persecuted or oppressed. Still, they remain vulnerable in social and economic terms, they face racist attitudes, and most of their traditional culture and way of life has disappeared. There are many reasons to shift to English, the majority language, and very few to stick to an Australian language. All or almost all these languages may be gone in a few generations.

In the United States and Canada the remaining Indian languages are in a similar predicament. In spite of certain attempts at revival it seems that most of them may vanish within a couple of generations. It is believed that there were around 300 languages when the Europeans arrived, and as late as the 1960s linguists estimated that about 200 of these languages were still spoken. In the last few decades, however, the number has declined rapidly as the last speakers of many languages have died. Their children, of course, speak English.

In Central and South America one may see a similar trend, but things have not advanced nearly as far. The young speakers of many Indian languages shift to Spanish or Portuguese in growing numbers. There are still several hundred languages left.

In Asia and in Europe there are many fewer languages, relatively speaking, as large languages have already been expanding for a long time, and have devoured most of the small languages a long time ago. Still quite a few things are happening. In the nineteenth century, Russia subjugated the whole of Siberia, which was inhabited by a large number of small groups of people with languages of their own. Most people in Siberia now speak Russian, and many of the small languages are endangered or disappearing.

In Europe there are only a few tens of small languages, next to nothing compared to the rest of the world. Most of these are declining rapidly; the situation of Gaelic has already been presented. The most spectacular case may be Irish, which is hardly used any more as a native spoken language among children, in spite of very strong support from the Irish government. There are several other cases, such as Sorbian (a Slavic language) in Germany, the Saami languages in northern Scandinavia, and so on. Although all these languages nowadays receive much more support than most languages in Africa or South America, they are still in a very precarious situation because of the overwhelming strength of the majority languages.

In Africa, the situation is different. There are perhaps 2,000 languages on the continent, and most of them are small by any standards. According to a survey made a few years ago around 200 languages are acutely threatened or are not actually in use any more. So in this continent as in others the number of languages decreases rapidly.

The difference is that speakers in Africa do not usually shift to a large European language such as English, French, or

Portuguese. These languages are very much present in Africa, as they are the former colonial languages. They are still official languages in almost all the former colonies, they are used in administration and in all higher education, and they serve daily as a means of oral and written communication for hundreds of millions of Africans. But the people who speak a small language do not shift to one of these. In the first place, there are no very large groups of first language speakers of European languages in Africa, except in South Africa. Secondly, the small languages are not found in the cities where the European languages are strong, but in the countryside. There they are subjected to pressure from some neighbouring language. Sometimes speakers shift from a very small language to one that is just a little larger, but important in the local environment. Quite often, though, they take up one of the languages that have grown strong in various states and regions during the twentieth century. In Tanzania and Kenya that means Swahili, in Zimbabwe it is Shona, in Nigeria either Hausa, Yoruba, or Igbo, and so on. In this way many languages disappear and a few relatively strong ones grow stronger at a rapid pace.

All this adds up to a guess that out of the 6,000 or so languages spoken at present, at least 1,000 will disappear in a couple of generations. If the trend continues, about half the languages spoken now may be gone in a hundred years.

As can be seen from the survey above, language extinction is rarely caused by a sudden catastrophe, in which all speakers die or are killed, although such things have indeed happened, for example on Tasmania when the Europeans arrived in the early eighteenth century. What usually happens, though, is that people shift from the language spoken by their parents to another language, and as a consequence they do not transmit the old language to their children. The basic phenomenon is language shift. Thus, in the future, more people will speak fewer languages.

However, it is not easy to know more precisely what will happen, and not all languages will have identical fates. Much depends on the speakers, as can be seen from the difference between two small languages in Africa.

SHIYEYI AND THIMBUKUSHU

In northern Botswana there is a large, remarkable wetland. The Okavango River flows inland towards the Kalahari Desert and finds no outlet but forms a big delta where the water evaporates in the hot and dry climate. This delta is very beautiful, and its nature has been little affected by humans. One may see elephants and lions, giraffes, and large herds of buffaloes. There are also some villages where people live as fishermen and small-scale farmers. In the most scenic spots, there are also small, exclusive lodges for tourists. Nowadays, the delta is a nature reserve.

The people who live in and around the delta belong to a number of groups speaking a variety of languages. The most numerous ones are the Wayeyi, who speak the Shiyeyi language. Possibly they are around 25,000 people. Another large group are the Hambukushu, who speak Thimbukushu; they may be 5,000 to 10,000. Many people also speak Setswana, the main language of Botswana. That language gains speakers, while the others are losing.

Shiyeyi and Thimbukushu are in a very similar situation, if seen through the eyes of an outsider. Both languages are spoken by small minorities in a remote corner of the country. Neither language is used in school, which is attended by most children. In the first few years Setswana is used, and later on the language of instruction becomes English. Neither of the small languages has been used as a written language except quite marginally.

However, the two languages are not moving in the same direction. Shiyeyi is losing speakers very swiftly. The children do not learn it as the first language any more, but possibly as a second language, and then not very well. Of the 25,000 people who consider themselves to be Wayeyi only about half actually speak Shiyeyi as their native language. The others are native speakers of Setswana and use Shiyeyi as a second language or not at all.

On the other hand, the Hambukushu do not seem to desert their language at all. Although they are fewer than the Wayeyi, their language is not threatened at present. The children learn it at home, and the parents continue using it in their daily lives.

This difference has nothing to do with external factors, but with traditions, history, and choices. The Wayeyi never had a strong societal organization and easily adapted to the new situation when the delta was conquered in the nineteenth century by the Batawana, a Setswana-speaking group. Also, they have traditionally been mobile and willing to work in distant places. Now they are often able to get well-paid jobs close to home in the tourist industry. Marriages outside the group are quite frequent. When formal education was becoming available a few decades ago they were eager to send their children to the new schools.

The Hambukushu have been self-governing for a long time, and live fairly closely together in a couple of areas. They are not particularly interested in formal education, but feel strongly about their own traditions. Their connections are very much within the group, so that they have far fewer contacts with outsiders than the Wayeyi have.

For a language, dissimilarities of this kind may make all the difference between continued existence and disappearance. When people choose which language to use they are not just guided by external pressures and material advantages. It is also important what they think is valuable and who they consider themselves to be.

THE DISAPPEARANCE OF LANGUAGES— GOOD OR BAD?

When young Wayeyi are asked what languages they use they say that they mostly use Setswana, and sometimes English, but almost never Shiyeyi. But if one asks them what they think about the Shiyeyi language it turns out that they think very highly of it and that they consider it important that it continues to be used, as it is an integral part of their own culture. Actually, the people who are least proficient in the language appreciate it the most.

It may seem that these people are irrational or insincere, but neither judgement is correct. The young ones identify with the group they belong to, the Wayeyi, as is normal for everyone to do. They know that the language is one of the main characteristics of the group and they appreciate it, which is just as natural.

The fact that they do not speak it much depends on circumstances that are not of their own making.

One of these circumstances is that the parents spoke mainly Setswana at home, possibly for reasons of convenience but perhaps out of consideration for their children. They probably valued Shiyeyi just as much, but thought that it was of overriding importance that their children learnt the language of the school as early as possible. If many parents act in the same way it may mean that the language disappears, although the individual parents or the individual children in no way wanted that to happen.

This seems to be the usual situation. A language vanishes not because the speakers want it to but in spite of the fact that they do not want it to. It also seems that the speakers themselves usually do not realize that their language is in danger until very late, when the young generation has already almost lost it. Some Wayeyi see this now. An association with the objective of furthering the language has been founded recently; one of its goals is to work out an orthography. It remains to be seen what will come out of this effort.

If the speakers almost always think it is a bad thing that their language dies, are there other people who want to murder it? The answer is yes, in many cases at least. In all states there are governments, and the great majority of governments believe it is an advantage to the country if there are few ethnic groups and few languages.

Partly this is because so many people believe that the ideal political organization is the nation state with just one ethnic group and one language. This idea became strong in Europe, where several states also developed in that direction, as has been seen above. In many of the states of the world, though, the reality is quite different. Partly the aversion of governments is also caused by the practical problems encountered in a multilingual community. It may be hard or impossible to organize elementary education in many languages. It is not possible to write laws and conduct discussions in parliament in many languages, and it may be impracticable to employ policemen and health personnel mastering a number of languages.

For these reasons state authorities almost always dislike all except one or two of a country's languages. Their main concern may be not with small minorities but with large ones, because they are politically dangerous. On the other hand, the small ones may often be shoved aside without political risks.

In Europe, nation states have been strong for a long time and so they have managed to eliminate many languages. Harsh methods were often employed. In countries such as France and Sweden, pupils could be severely punished not so long ago if they spoke their native language rather than the official one during breaks in school. In most European states minority languages are now tolerated and sometimes even supported. This may possibly be because of a more developed concern for the rights of minorities, but more probably it reflects the fact that these minorities are not perceived as a threat any more.

In Botswana, where Shiyeyi and Thimbukushu are spoken, there is one majority language, Setswana, and about twenty other languages. Most of these have very few speakers. Even if the government wanted to, it could not possibly provide elementary education in all those languages, or provide any other meaningful service in them. They are left out of the radical changes of society, for there is nothing else to do. No languages are actively repressed, as was the case in Europe, but they are also not supported in any way. If they cease to exist there will undoubtedly be fewer problems for many government officials.

In addition to the speakers and the governments, there are others who express opinions on this matter. Researchers in linguistics and anthropology have realized what is happening, and are of course very upset about the fact that hundreds of languages are disappearing. Each one of them is a cultural product, formed by the experiences and the creativity of many generations of speakers. However, there are different ideas about what should be done. Some researchers feel that one should alert public opinion and the speakers themselves to what is going on and try to reverse the trend. Others feel it is the business of researchers to describe what is happening and to document the disappearing languages in so far as it is possible, but not to intervene.

Probably it does not matter very much what researchers do or do not do. Under the social and economic conditions that prevail today languages will continue to disappear. Few people actually like the fact that it is happening, but there are such substantial advantages in shifting from a small language to a larger one that very many will do it themselves or encourage their children to do it.

Chapter 12
The Heyday of English

A traveller in Europe 100 years ago could expect to find people speaking a foreign language only in international hotels and tourist resorts and among a quite small group of well-educated people. The foreign language they might be acquainted with varied from country to country. In Central and Eastern Europe, from Romania to Sweden, people would know some German. In Italy and Portugal, French was understood in many places, and in countries around the North Sea, such as Norway and the Netherlands, there was a fair chance of finding someone speaking English.

Nowadays, a stranger in a European country stands a very good chance of meeting someone who has mastered a foreign language to some extent wherever a need for communication may arise. Furthermore, among younger people at least, the language is English in the great majority of cases.

During the last 100 years, then, there have been two great changes. In the first place, many more people have learnt an internationally useful foreign language, in Europe and in many other parts of the world. In the second place, there was a choice among several languages a century ago, but now the foreign language (or the first foreign language) that is learnt is almost always English. Those two things of course are related to a certain extent, but they really have very different causes.

To begin with the increase in the learning of languages; this has to do with the fact that both school education and international contacts are more important in the lives of most people nowadays than they were 100 years ago. When industrial societies emerged in Europe, and a little later in other parts of the world, one of the consequences was an increasing demand for education. General elementary education for all children became a reality in many countries during the nineteenth century, and during the twentieth century almost all countries have been able to offer their children a few years of school. In the most affluent countries many or most attend school for ten or twelve years, and a third or more may go on to some kind of college or university. All this means that there are ample opportunities to include language instruction in the curricula in many countries.

Contacts across linguistic as well as national borders are much more frequent now than 100 years ago. At that time, most Europeans still lived in the countryside and worked on farms. Most of the others were industrial workers. Only a tiny percentage had any reason ever to use a foreign language in their profession. Few people travelled abroad, except for those who emigrated to America, but that was mostly a one-way trip. It is true that there were substantial linguistic minorities in almost all European countries, but in most cases the minorities lived in fairly restricted areas. Minority-language speakers had to learn the majority language, but majority-language speakers did not learn a minority language. Thus most people knew only one language.

Nowadays most Europeans live in cities, and more people are employed in the service and communication sectors than in industrial production, not to speak of agriculture. This means many more casual encounters, including with people from other countries. Most people have been abroad, some for long periods. Many have to use one or more foreign languages in their work. In their leisure time, all except English-speaking people hear a foreign language—English—almost daily in pop music, in TV news reports, and in many other contexts. Everyday life in most European countries is not monolingual but multilingual.

The same is true for many, probably most countries all over the world. Everywhere people move into cities, and almost everywhere education is longer than it used to be and includes at least one foreign language. Generally, contacts between countries and between linguistic areas are increasing, and more people migrate from one country to another. The consequences vary, depending on the local circumstances, but almost everywhere the net result is that more people learn at least one foreign language and fewer remain monolingual.

The exceptions are found in the countries where the majority language is so large and dominating that all contacts can be handled in that language. To a great extent this is true for Chinese in China and Spanish in Latin America, as well as a number of other large languages. The ones who are least liable to need a foreign language are majority speakers of English in the United States, Britain, and several other countries. As a matter of fact, though, language contacts are becoming more frequent even there. The United States now has a significant Spanish-speaking minority that did not exist thirty years ago. Britain has had considerable immigration from many countries, and contacts within the European Union are more extensive than earlier.

So, monolingualism is retreating in favour of multilingualism all over the world. Why is the second language so often English?

FRENCH, GERMAN, RUSSIAN, ENGLISH

French secured a position as an international language in the seventeenth century, as has been mentioned above. This had much to do with the cultural and political strength of France, especially during the long reign of Louis XIV (1643–1715). France remained very influential throughout the eighteenth century, but it lost much of its political power as a result of the Napoleonic wars. Since 1815, France has still been a significant country in Europe, but it is no longer outstanding.

All the same, French kept much of its status as the preferred international language for a long time. It remained the language of diplomacy throughout the nineteenth century and some way into the twentieth. When international postal services on a regular basis were introduced in the nineteenth century, French became the common postal language. It also kept a strong position as a language of science.

French met with competition in Europe, however, first from German. After the unification of Germany under Prussia and the French–German war of the early 1870s, Germany was the politically dominating power for a number of decades. At the same time, the country advanced fast in the fields of technology and science. It became desirable to know German, primarily in the adjacent smaller countries but also to some extent in the other large European countries and in the United States.

However, Germany did not remain on top long enough for German to obtain high international status. After the two world wars Germany had lost all political influence, and most of its edge in technology and science. It is true that the country recovered swiftly, but that has not resulted in a leading part on the international stage.

Those parts were reserved for the winners of the Second World War, the United States and the Soviet Union. From 1945 to 1990, the world was dominated by their military might, their rivalry, and their aspirations to power. During the same period the world economy was booming, as well as world population. Education expanded everywhere, and so did international exchange of many kinds.

English and Russian, the languages of the two superpowers, naturally profited from this situation. English had a comfortable lead from the start, as will be discussed presently. However, Russian advanced rapidly for several decades. It became the first foreign language in school education in many countries belonging to the Russian sphere of influence, and it grew important in technology and science. The Soviet Union also insisted that Russian should be used as much as possible in diplomatic relations and in international co-operation. Around 1980 it seemed reasonable to believe that the world was being split into two main linguistic spheres, one using English as its common language and the other using Russian.

However, when the Soviet Union collapsed in 1990 Russian lost its international standing at an amazing speed. In eastern Europe and in other parts of the world where it was a foreign language in schools it is mostly not taught any more. Russia lags far behind in technology and science, and important new results are hardly published in Russian nowadays. At present, Russian may possibly compete with French or Spanish on an international ranking list of languages. English, on the other hand, has a privileged position as the preferred international language, without any serious competition at present. The reasons can be found in a number of historical developments that have all been to the advantage of the English language.

THE TIME OF ENGLISH

From the sixteenth century onwards, a few languages of Europe have gradually become the most important ones for communications between language groups, as conquests, business, and colonization promoted them in large parts of the world.

Britain turned out to be the most successful imperial power. At the beginning of the twentieth century it wielded political power in India, in large parts of Africa south of the Sahara, in Canada, in Australia, in several trading centres in East Asia, and in a large number of smaller possessions elsewhere. The English language was strong in all these areas. At that time, English was an important European language, but hardly the leading one, and was also used more for international contacts in the rest of the world than any other language.

After the two world wars, Germany was crushed and France was much weakened. But Britain also had spent most of its resources, and the time of the empire was gone. The political and economic lead was taken by the United States, an English-speaking country outside Europe.

The English language was boosted all over Europe through the Marshall Plan, the presence of American troops, and so on. At the same time the new leading power took advantage of the fact that its language, English, already had a strong presence in all the countries that belonged or had belonged to the British Empire. The combination furthered the spread of English in an unprecedented way.

In the diplomatic world, English gradually succeeded French in the course of the twentieth century. At the foundation of the United Nations in 1945, not only French, but a total of five languages, of which four were European ones, became officially recognized: English, French, Spanish, Russian, and Chinese (Arabic has been added later). The headquarters is in New York. In practice, English has become the most important language within the organization.

There are reasons other than the political ones for the success of English. The United States assumed its leading position after 1945 not only because of military strength, but also as a consequence of its very strong economy. It was based on industrial and technological progress. As early as the beginning of the twentieth century, America took the lead in a number of key industries. A couple of them have meant very much for international contacts: telecommunications and aviation. In both areas the United States got an edge, and to a large extent they retain their advantage. Civil aviation was first developed there, and the language of this large international line of business has been English from the start. The same is true for telephones, radio, and television.

The film industry is a special case. The fact that Hollywood took the lead had no great linguistic significance in the silent film era, but it became very important when sound-film was invented. The American film and television industries now convey an enormous amount of spoken English to people all over the world, especially in small and/or poor countries where dubbing is too expensive.

Popular vocal music, which constitutes another branch of the media business, also contributes to the spread of English. Singers and songwriters such as John Lennon or Bob Dylan may have reached larger audiences all over the world than any performers before them. This is not only because of their artistic qualities but also a consequence of the fact that English has been the main language in the world of commercial music since the American invention of the phonograph.

The traditional means of electronic communication, the telephone, can be used by speakers of any language. However, when international telephone calls became a reality in everyday life, which was in the 1960s in most industrialized countries, large numbers of people wanted to use this opportunity for immediate contacts in their business. But in order to talk people must use a common language, and this meant in practice that speakers of many other languages had to learn English well. More recently introduced media, especially e-mail and other data services via the Internet can be used, in principle, for all written languages (which excludes all the small languages without a written norm). In practice, the international contacts are mostly in English, and that language is also an indispensable tool for the millions of technicians, programmers, and others who maintain the net, service the computers, and so on.

In the field of science the United States became significant as early as before the First World War, and in the course of the twentieth century it took the lead in most fields. Britain also performed strongly in some areas. A result of this has been that in practice English has become the language of all published works of primary importance in one area after another. During the last few decades, and especially after the demise of the Soviet Union, English has attained such dominance that it is almost *the* language of science. There is no real precedent to that. Latin had a similar position up to a couple of centuries ago, but after all it was used mainly in Europe.

Another important area in which English has conquered is the world of finance. Money transactions and stock markets provide a living for many people and are important for many more. The largest international centres for those activities are New York and London, and no one in the business can well afford not to understand the language used in those places.

It would be very easy to list several other areas that already use mainly English, or are moving in that direction. As English is becoming necessary in more fields, more people have to learn the language, and when so many know it already it is becoming even easier to introduce it in yet another area. At this point in time the advance of English seems irresistible.

There is one important area, though, where English is not very prominent. It has no strong link to any of the great religions of the world. It is true that much missionary work is done by people from the United States and Britain, but it is a matter of spreading Protestant Christianity of various shades, all subscribing to the idea that the religious message is to be transmitted in people's native language. Therefore, the missionaries do not in principle propagate the English language, even if their activities may sometimes have that effect. English is in no way connected with a faith, as Arabic is linked to Muslim religion or Latin became a vehicle of Christianity.

It should also be noted that the actual number of speakers of English as a first language is not extremely high. The latest estimate is 341 million people; this is similar to the figures for Spanish (358 million) and Hindi (366 million), and very much below that for Mandarin Chinese, a language spoken by around 874 million people. The figures are to be regarded as crude estimates, but they show the relations between those languages quite clearly. English is different from the others in that more people speak it as a second language or as a foreign language, but the total number of these is just unknown. Guesses range from 200 million to perhaps 1,000 million people. In any case, the total number of people who know some English is almost certainly lower than the number of native speakers of Mandarin Chinese.

To sum up, English has become the leading international language because of three rather different developments. First, the language acquired a strong position in large parts of the world as Britain built and maintained its empire from the seventeenth through to the early twentieth century. Secondly, the United

States gained a leading position in technology, economy, and politics in the first part of the twentieth century, and still retains this status. Thirdly, industry, communications, and international relations developed in such a way in the twentieth century that a common language was much more in demand than before. English was there to fill the need, while the other European languages had been pushed aside for different reasons.

IMAGES OF ENGLISH

As the prominent position of English is caused by the three factors mentioned, the attitudes to English among people outside the English-speaking countries may vary accordingly. English may be seen as a language for communication all over the world, or as a tool for the imperialist ambitions of the United States, or as a colonial heritage. All these views are justified to some extent. The different opinions tend to prevail in different parts of the world.

In countries outside the direct spheres of influence of the United States and Britain people often stress the advantages of using one international language in contacts with many linguistic areas. People who speak a small language as their native tongue appreciate that one other language opens up opportunities for contacts in many directions. For this reason it is becoming ever more important to learn English as a second language in most countries of the world.

However, this is not without problems. All languages are expressions or embodiments of a particular human culture. In this sense, no language is neutral, even if some people wish to believe so. English is a European language with a specific history, a literature, and a structuring of the world. It is also linked to several states, one of which is extremely influential all over the world. A person who learns English also assimilates important parts of English culture and is influenced by it. She or he is liable to prefer contacts with English-speaking countries, and thus continue to receive impulses from the same cultural sphere. If most people speaking a certain language are in this situation the total impact from English may become overwhelming.

This is what has happened in many countries during the last few decades. The direct signs of influence on a language are first a very large number of loanwords from English; such words are adapted to the sound system of the language. Secondly, non-adapted English words may intrude in the speech of many people. Thirdly, parts of sentences or even whole sentences in English may be interspersed with ordinary speech in the language.

Still more important, however, is the fact that English tends to be used as the language of communication in certain contexts. In multinational companies, English may be the spoken and written language in Amsterdam and Rome as well as in Chicago. At universities in many parts of the world, advanced seminars and graduate courses are regularly conducted in English, as researchers from several countries may participate, and English is almost always their only common language. This situation is beginning to provoke questions about the long-term prospects of many languages, even large ones, in face of the competition from English.

Some states openly resist the English influence. A notable instance is France, which does not willingly accept that English has usurped the international position that French used to have. Now, French is protected in its home country by all available means. This is fairly natural in a nation state with aspirations to power. But even small and comparatively powerless nation states, such as the Scandinavian ones, may feel that this is something of a threat. Whenever English acquires a new function, that function is taken away from the national language.

Countries such as India, Nigeria, and many others that used to belong to the British Empire are in a special situation. When they became independent in the decades following the Second World War all these countries had administrations and school systems that functioned in English. In most of the countries this is still the case. This means in most cases that English is the language of instruction at least in advanced education, and in some countries even in elementary school. For several reasons it has not been possible or realistic to make a change. In the first place, school systems and official administrations have considerable inertia and are not easy to change radically at any time. Secondly, there have not been any good models for alternative administrations and schools, and new ones are not easily invented. Thirdly, most of the former colonies are multilingual, and to stick to English has often been the only viable strategy to avoid divisive fights about language issues.

For these reasons English remains strong in most of these countries. In many of them, including gigantic India, English actually has a stronger foothold now than it had at independence. The general level of education is higher now and national and international contacts across linguistic boundaries have become more frequent. For that reason more people learn English and use it.

At the same time, English is associated with the old colonial power in these countries, and that of course is a negative connotation. But as English remains so strong in the schools, in fact often much stronger than any native language of the country, a large part of school education really is an initiation into English culture. This is most true for those who get the highest education.

The ties between those countries and Britain are of varying kinds; on the whole the relations are neither very close nor uniformly cordial. However, there are special channels for education, in particular for education in English. The British Council provides teachers who are native speakers of English, and it distributes textbooks and other material for teaching. The universities in Cambridge and Oxford administer examinations that are used for awarding certificates at the advanced school level in many countries. In this way Britain still wields considerable influence on education in many of the former colonies.

In Britain there has been some ideologically motivated discussion about this fact. Some believe the activities of the British Council and similar organizations amount to "linguistic imperialism." It is probably true that some highly placed people in Britain feel that language education is a good way to keep and strengthen the ties with the former colonies. But in so far as this is an attempt at imperialism it is not very impressive. Britain can no longer assert itself globally by economic, political, or military means. Rather, it is a country that wants the income it may get through the textbooks and the native English teachers.

Naturally, what Britain does is also not very important for the standing of English in the former colonies. As has been shown, quite different forces work for the language. A tangible proof of this is that English is gaining ground even in states that once were colonies of other European powers. Namibia was a German colony for a few decades and after that was administered for about seventy years by South Africa; the colonial languages were first German and then Afrikaans, which was promoted very forcibly by the South African authorities. After independence in 1990, the new government has settled for English as official language and school language. Mozambique used to be completely dominated by Portuguese, but a growing number of people in leading positions now master English. Many young persons know English even in the Central African Republic, a former French colony still more or less supervised by France. In all those cases, Britain is completely irrelevant.

The United States is a different matter. The country has a cultural influence almost everywhere, through film, TV, music, and in other ways, and it is a major player in economy and politics. American companies prefer English in all countries. Of course the power of the United States is important for the spread of English. In fact, one may describe the spread as one aspect of the economic and cultural imperialism of that country, if one chooses to use such a terminology.

However, governmental authorities of the United States are not spending much time or money on the promotion of English in other countries. There are libraries, cultural centres, and the like in some places, but not much more than that. The political activities of the country have not necessarily furthered the

English language very much. True, there are or have been American military bases in many places, and that certainly has contributed to some extent to the spread of English in such countries as Iceland and Germany, but it has hardly been of major importance.

Further, the countries closest to the United States are not the ones that have adopted English without reservations. In Latin America in general English is not exceptionally strong, and seems to be losing ground. In Mexico, for example, there certainly is some English in the school curriculum, but less than in many European countries, and very much less than in such countries as Kenya or Nigeria. Political pressure from the United States seems not to have led to increased interest in English, but rather the reverse.

The conclusion is that English is not furthered very much by the activities of Britain and the United States. Britain cannot do much, and the United States does not do much.

Generally speaking, if English is seen as closely linked to Britain and the United States, that does not further its use as an international language. In those countries where those links are manifest the language meets with considerable resistance. The image of English that contributes most to its growth is that of a supranational language for international communication. At present that image prevails with many people, and English is gaining ground.

For how long will this be going on? No one knows, of course. It is interesting to speculate, though, and such speculation is the topic of the final chapter.

Chapter 13
And Then?

Predictions about a distant future should be met with scepticism; it is hard enough to know what is going to happen next week. All the same, this chapter is about what may happen to the languages of the world. As developments in this area are comparatively slow it is necessary to look quite far ahead if one wants to see significant changes.

Of course I do not believe that it is possible to foresee what is actually going to take place. Still there is a point in bringing up the issue. I think I have shown in this book that there are connections between society and language: certain features in society will tend to favour certain types of linguistic developments. If that is so, it is indeed possible to make predictions about what will happen to languages if societies develop in a certain way. That is what I try to do in this chapter. For that reason all predictions are conditional: if history goes in this direction, then languages will be affected in this way. This may give some food for thought, and is at the same time a kind of summary of what has been suggested in different contexts in previous chapters.

And Then?

The first prediction is easy and depressing. If the human species becomes extinct, human languages will vanish at the same time, and there is nothing more to be said. What is treated below is the possible situation at three points in the future, provided that the species is not extinguished.

IN TWO HUNDRED YEARS

If someone 200 years ago had tried to predict the language situation in our time, the chances of a correct result would have been extremely small. The present political conditions could not possibly have been foreseen. No one could reasonably have guessed, for example, that the British colonies on the east coast of North America that had recently declared themselves independent would develop into a leading world power within 150 years. Also, there was no reason to believe that the world's population would become seven or eight times larger in 200 years; nothing like that had ever happened before. Again, no one could really have conjectured that this giant population would also live much longer, on average.

The situation is in no way easier now. For that reason I will just try to say what might happen to languages under certain specified conditions. I start with the assumption that people continue living under social and economic conditions that are more or less similar to the ones that obtain now, and that the trends that can be observed at present are not reversed. This means, among other things, that states will still exist, and that many of them will be nation states. Later, I will make some comments on the more probable alternative that there will be very large upheavals of one kind or another.

In the first scenario, then, most people will certainly speak one of a small number of large languages, just like now. The small languages will face difficulties as long as the world is approximately like now. If the present trend continues, two or three thousand languages out of the five or seven thousand that exist now may have disappeared in 200 years. Possibly the process may be even swifter, if large languages and states become even more powerful. In that case, the number of surviving languages may be counted in the hundreds rather than in the thousands in two centuries.

What speaks against this large-scale extinction is the fact that most people actually wish very strongly that their native tongue should be preserved. In some cases, mostly in Europe, much is being done to preserve and revitalize a language. An example is Welsh, the Celtic language spoken in Wales. If most countries that have many languages now become more similar to Britain in terms of economy and general education there may possibly be similar developments on a large scale. So far, however, there are few signs that this is going to happen. Also, it remains uncertain how much such measures mean for the long-term survival of a language.

The languages that will go first are the ones that the speakers do not feel proud about, that have no written forms and no names of their own. This is largely true for the Khoisan languages that were discussed in Chapter 1, and also for many Creole languages. These and many others may disappear quite soon.

And Then?

Languages that are now spoken by several million people, that are established as written languages, and that have some position in education, or are at least recognized as existing languages in a country, will hardly disappear in 200 years, generally speaking. Under all assumptions, it is probable that in some places there will be wars, large migrations or other reversals that may spell the end for a whole people. But except in the case of such large catastrophes, 200 years will hardly be enough for large groups to shift completely to another language under conditions that are similar to the present ones. Two hundred years means something like eight generations, and even a very rapid language shift for a small group takes about three generations before it is completed. A large population with a well-established language will not shift to another one quickly if they are not subjected to very strong pressure.

This is of course even truer for languages that are supported by political power. If nation states continue to exist more or less as now their national languages will almost certainly remain. It is in the nature of nation states to favour one language. Some states, especially in Africa, may actually become more like nation states in that they will strongly support one language and suppress a number of others.

However, even many national languages are used less now than they were a couple of generations ago in certain functions. English is employed much more now than earlier in countries such as Sweden or the Netherlands, especially in the media and in certain areas of working life. As a consequence of that and of the fact that almost all children in Sweden and the Netherlands learn English in school, Swedish and Dutch are also strongly influenced by English. Will this continue, or even accelerate?

This really is not one question, but two. The first is whether languages such as Swedish and Dutch, and most other languages, will be influenced by an international language in the future too, and the other is whether this international language will be English.

The first question is somewhat easier than the second. Under the assumption that no very great calamities will occur, international contacts will remain strong, and will probably grow stronger. Research, technology, business, and other activities become much easier if there are generally acknowledged languages for international contacts. Such languages, or at least one such language, will be used in the future too. If the world does not change radically school education in most countries will include instruction in some international language.

Whether English will retain its position is a completely different matter. Several concurrent forces caused its unprecedented success in the twentieth century. An important one was the political and economic power of the United States. One of the lessons of history is that such matters change. Two centuries may be time enough for several states to rise to superpowers and then fall back again. Of course it is also possible that the United States will keep the lead, or that the next leader will also be an English-speaking country, but neither alternative seems particularly probable.

What will be the consequence for English as an international language? In the first place, it will have to compete with the language of the next superpower, whether it is Chinese, Spanish,

Russian, or some even more unpredictable one. That would mean a situation similar to the one that obtained just a few decades ago, when Russian still competed with English. In a longer perspective, a new international language may of course take over all international functions from English.

If that happens, it will probably require considerable time. One of the reasons for the strength of English is that it is used as the language of instruction in many former colonies. This has been so for generations, and a change would require several decades. Also, many other countries would have to change curricula in order to introduce another first foreign language, and that is a slow process. On the other hand, real change may be surprisingly fast, as could be seen in countries such as Hungary and the Czech republic after the fall of the Soviet Union. Russian used to be the most important foreign language but is now already far behind English and German. This is because many adults may learn a language or improve their competence in it if a need arises.

Much that is written in English is not translated into any other language, especially within research and technology, but in many other areas too. For that reason it would be necessary for scientists and for many others to learn both English and a new international language during a long transition period.

To see what may happen to English one can consider the decline of Latin and of French. The Roman Empire ceased to exist in the west in the fifth century, but Latin played an important role as an international language even a thousand years later. France acquired its strong position in the seventeenth century, and French remained an international language in certain areas about a century after France had lost that position.

English is extremely strong as an international language now, but it is still much more like French than like Latin. Latin was the only well-developed written language, and it had a monopoly in education. English is the most successful among several other well-established languages, each one of which could fulfil the functions that English has assumed without any difficulty. Each of these languages has a strong base in at least one nation state.

So, in my view English will probably be less dominant in 200 years than it is now, as it is unlikely that it will be favoured by the political situation for such a long time. However, it may possibly retain some of its standing for other reasons.

At present, English is most popular in countries that do not feel threatened by the United States or Britain. There, people tend to appreciate the language as a useful tool in international dealings, disregarding its national base. If all English-speaking states became powerless, relatively speaking, the language might perhaps grow more popular in some contexts precisely because it would be free from political liabilities. However, this effect should not be overestimated. If China becomes the world centre for research and economy for a long time, contacts between China and the rest of the world will not indefinitely be mediated through English.

English is used as a native language in many parts of the world. Already, the spoken geographical variants of the language are fairly dissimilar. They will become more divergent because of the nature of language change, unless contacts between continents become much closer than they are now. In 200 years it may be quite difficult for people from different continents to understand each other. If the common written language is preserved everywhere it will also be even further removed from all the different pronunciations than it is at present. The consequences of this are not easy to predict, but it may become more problematic to use English as an international language if there are great variations within the language.

In summary, I speculate that many small languages will disappear, that one or a few languages will be used in international contexts, that English is not necessarily one of those languages, and that the remaining large or fairly large languages will exist more or less like now.

All this, however, is based on the assumption that no major trends are reversed. If that happens, it is even more difficult to predict the outcome, but one may imagine a number of possible scenarios.

One is that a small number of states seize political and economic hegemony over the whole world, each over a part of it, and try to force their languages on all people under their sway. During the Cold War people often imagined a future of this kind, but at present the idea seems much less popular.

In such a situation, it is not very probable that an attempt to eradicate other languages quickly by coercion would be successful. People who are subjected to what they feel is occupation or aggression tend to stick to their own culture and language very stubbornly. On the other hand, in the long run languages may give way in face of competition and vanish gradually. This happened in the Roman Empire on a large scale, it happened in East Sutherland on a much smaller scale, and it has happened on many other occasions. However, it takes considerable time. The national languages in use at present are mostly strong enough to hold their own for a long time. Even if the putative conquerors started tomorrow, there would hardly be time for very radical changes in 200 years, if one discounts outright genocide and similar methods.

Another possible long-term trend is the opposite one. Nation states now show some signs of weakness, at least in Europe. Smaller entities such as regions grow stronger. Suppose that most nation states dissolve into less extensive units. What would happen to languages?

In most parts of the world this would not make much of a difference, at least not in a couple of hundred years. If the United States were dissolved, the fifty states would probably all stick to English. If Germany, France, and Spain were transformed into many regions most of them certainly would opt for German, French, and Spanish, respectively, as their languages. A few regions would probably settle for another language, for example Catalan in Catalonia. However, it is not likely that German regions would make a local dialect their regional language. Germany was politically fragmented up to a century and a half ago, but a common written language and a common norm for spoken language could still develop.

In some parts of the world it would mean much more for languages if the present states disintegrated. The African states with very many languages might become several independent units, each one with much fewer languages and one main language. In Russia, a number of the linguistic minorities might become majorities in their own regions. In this way, a fairly large number of languages would obtain a more secure position than their present one. However, at present there are no sure indications that anything like this is going to occur.

And Then?

All these scenarios start from the assumption that economic and social conditions will become better or at least approximately equal to the present ones. However, the future may have a number of catastrophes in store. There may be very great wars, or economic and social collapse because of deterioration of the environment, or new ravaging diseases, or a combination of these and other calamities. What will befall the languages?

It is actually possible to say something about that, at least in general terms. When societies are under great strain a number of services break down. Schools may cease to exist; communications with the rest of the world may become sporadic or non-existent. People are left to fend for themselves at the place where they happen to be. The average lifespan becomes very much shorter.

It is reasonable to believe that in places where such things occur languages will change fast. If knowledge of written language disappears or becomes irrelevant, and people are not able to travel or to use electronic means of communication any more, the function of language will be restricted to local contacts. This was more or less what happened in western Europe during the centuries after the fall of the Roman Empire. The result was that a number of mutually unintelligible languages developed out of Latin. If things become bad enough the same may happen to English or Spanish.

How long this would take is not easy to say. It is unusual for languages to change radically in a couple of centuries, but in certain cases new languages may be created within that time-span, as can be seen from Creole languages and Afrikaans. It seems, though, that such swift change comes about only if there are people who speak several languages to begin with. Then, a common language much different from all the original ones may appear in a short time. Further, change is probably faster if the average person has a short life, as that will reduce the amount of contact between generations and thereby harm the transmission of language. If the isolated groups are small that may also mean a faster rate of change.

Under hardship the organization of states breaks down, as has been seen recently in countries such as Sierra Leone and Somalia. When this happens, many of the forces adverse to small languages cease to exist. In a world where anarchy is widespread, the many small languages will not be ousted by larger languages. However, many of them may disappear all the same, as all the speakers may die.

So, in a world of disasters the number of languages will probably rise again, at least in the long run. Societal order, schools, and communications tend to diminish the number of languages, isolation and anarchy tend to augment it. Both are long-term trends, but after a few centuries the effects will be large.

In summary, even if it is not possible to foretell the future, one can say a great deal about what will happen to languages under different conditions. So far, the perspective has been short, in relation to the normal rate of change of languages. A few things can also be said about what may come to pass over a longer period of time.

IN TWO THOUSAND YEARS

It can be stated with some confidence that if there are human beings around two millennia from now, they will speak languages of the same kind as the ones that are used now. The thousands of languages spoken at present have a large number of common features that are related to very specialized and genetically inherited capabilities of humans. The species will not change genetically in as short a period as 2,000 years. For that reason people will speak languages like ours at that time.

A few other things can also be safely asserted. First, no language spoken at that time will be very close to any language that is spoken now. It is quite possible that there will be languages that carry the same names, that there are languages called "English" or "Español" (the Spanish word for "Spanish") or "Elliniki" (the Greek word for "Greek") by the speakers. The last name has already been used for a language for more than 2,000 years, and there is no reason why it could not be in use 2,000 years from now. But the spoken language will continue to change. Present-day Greek is very dissimilar to the language spoken by Plato, and if Greek is still spoken in 2,000 years it will be quite different from now. All languages that are used are also changed.

Secondly, the languages that will be spoken at that time will include many elements derived from languages spoken now. Languages are not invented; they change. Not even Creole languages start from scratch, but contain very many ingredients from other languages. This will almost certainly remain so in the future. Two thousand years is a long time, but for historical linguists it is often possible to reconstruct what must have happened that far back in time. The changes during a period of that length do not make a language unrecognizable to a specialist.

Which languages will provide material for future ones is anyone's guess. From a statistical point of view the most likely ones are those that have many speakers now, such as Chinese, English, Hindi, or Spanish, but history and statistics are not always close friends. It may be that a language such as Icelandic, used as a national language on a comparatively isolated island, may change less than most other languages; it certainly has changed little in the last thousand years. But this is of course merely speculation.

It is also rather pointless to conjecture how many languages there will be in two millennia from now. It has been maintained above that this is dependent on politics, communications, education, and so on. There is no way of knowing anything at all about such matters 2,000 years in advance.

An extreme alternative may be discussed, though. It has been shown above that the number of languages has diminished from one millennium to the next throughout the time we can survey. The largest language at present is used by many more people than the total population on earth 2,000 years ago. How probable is it that all people talk one single language 2,000 years from now?

This is conceivable, but only if a number of conditions are met. All people must have frequent and extended contacts, they should want to identify with humanity rather than with a subgroup of any kind, and they have to have very explicit language norms that they also transmit very efficiently to the young. This is perfectly possible if, at that time, the human population is small and inhabits only a restricted area somewhere on the globe. If there are billions of people, spread all over the surface of earth, as is the case now, different languages will most probably remain in various areas, or else new languages will develop even if the whole world should have become monolingual at some point in time.

For languages will serve a double purpose in the future too. We transmit messages through the language, but the language also defines us as members of a group. New groups arise constantly, and with them new needs to show where one belongs. This is one of the reasons why languages change constantly. Through this mechanism, large languages always split up into dialects and later into separate languages unless there are strong counteracting forces. Those counteracting forces—communications, a strong state, a written language, and so on—have become more significant with time. But they will never eliminate the human need for a basic linguistic identity, and if the external forces grow weaker, the languages multiply. For this reason I do not believe that the world can have only one language for any extended period.

In 2,000 years there may well be written languages of the same kind that are used now. They were invented more than 2,000 years ago and have proved very versatile. It seems improbable that all humans should give up writing, even though independent writing systems have indeed been extinguished, for example when the Maya culture disappeared.

It is less easy to say which kind of writing will be used at that time. At present alphabetic writing systems are used for most languages of the world, and such systems have figured prominently in this book. However, Chinese is written with a system that uses one character for each word, in principle, and that language is used by one-fifth of the population on earth. Japanese can be written in several ways, and one of the systems is based on the principle of one character for each syllable. All three types of writing are quite functional and are used by many people. No one knows whether all three will remain or one of them will gain the upper hand. It is also quite possible that someone invents a still better way to represent spoken language. I am not thinking of recordings; they have been around for a long time now, and are in no way a substitute for writing.

One reason to think that written languages will look more or less like they do now is the fact that so far they have proved extremely tenacious. The Chinese system has changed little in more than 3,000 years, and Modern Greek is written with an alphabet that has been used for almost as long. The Romance languages, originating from Latin, are written with the Latin alphabet invented more than 2,500 years ago, and so are many other languages, including English. One reason for this absence of change is that people who have spent all the time necessary to be able to read and write in a language normally oppose all innovations. A change would mean much extra work, and it may make it impossible for later generations to read old documents. For that reason, radical alternatives are very rarely successful.

IN TWO MILLION YEARS

To see the end of the history of languages one has to look very far ahead. Again, this is under the assumption that the species will not be extinct. It probably will be, in my opinion; a species that has altered the biosystem in which it lives so drastically since its appearance is likely to suffer severely from the long-term effects of those changes. But supposing that our descendants survive all future crises, what will their languages be like? Somewhat arbitrarily, I have settled for 2 million years from now. Two million years ago is the most distant period that has been seriously suggested for the beginnings of human language.

It is completely certain that if any human languages are spoken at that time there will be no elements that can be derived from any language used now. In just 10,000 years languages are transformed beyond recognition. In 2 million years this would happen a couple of hundred times.

Other things would happen too. Our ancestors 2 million years ago were fairly different from us for genetic reasons. The species has developed, and one of the developments was that the capacity for language was enhanced. In 2 million years, many new genetic changes will have occurred. From the present species, several different species may have evolved, differing from each other in their linguistic capacity, for example.

That will be the end of the history of languages. It does not matter whether the new creatures acquire other and more advanced capacities, beyond our understanding, or become silent. If they do not speak languages that have the basic features required by our mental and physical qualities they do not belong to our species. Humans became human when they started talking like we do. When they do not speak like us they will not be human any more.

Suggestions for Further Reading

Below are some suggestions for further reading about various matters, and references to the sources for specialized information.

The book contains a large number of allusions to well-known events and persons in history and literature. More information about these can easily be found in standard encyclopedias or handbooks, such as *Encyclopaedia Britannica* or *The Oxford Encyclopedia of World History*.

For general information about linguistic matters an excellent source is David Crystal, *The Cambridge Encyclopedia of Language*, 2nd edn. (Cambridge: Cambridge University Press, 1997). A more comprehensive work is William Bright, *International Encyclopedia of Linguistics* (4 vols.; Oxford: Oxford University Press, 1991–2), which includes extensive discussions of the language groups of the world, with lists of most languages. For information about the languages used in each country of the world, an indispensable work is Barbara E. Grimes, *Ethnologue: Languages of the World*, 14th edn. (Dallas: Summer Institute of Linguistics (SIL), 2000). The work is also available (in the 13th edn.) on Internet, at the address: www.sil.org/ethnologue, last accessed 7 May 2001.

There does not seem to exist any previous attempt to write a general history of languages, except for my book in Swedish, *Språken och historien* (1997); the present volume is a much altered and updated version of that work.

1. Languages before History

For the origin of language, facts are scarce, but the amount of literature enormous. A few titles of interest are S. Jones *et al.*, *The Cambridge Encyclopedia of Human Evolution* (Cambridge: Cambridge University Press, 1992); P. Mellars and C. Stringer, *The Human Revolution*

(Edinburgh: Edinburgh University Press, 1989); Robin Dunbar, *Grooming, Gossip and the Evolution of Language* (London: Faber & Faber Ltd., 1996); Andrew Carstairs-McCarthy, *The Origins of Complex Language* (Oxford: Oxford University Press, 1999); *Approaches to the Evolution of Language: Social and Cognitive Bases*, ed. James R. Hurford *et al.* (Cambridge: Cambridge University Press, 1998); *The Evolution of Culture: An Interdisciplinary View*, ed. Robin Dunbar *et al.* (Edinburgh: Edinburgh University Press, 1999).

On San languages, little has been written. A short general survey in English is found in Oswin R. A. Köhler, "Khoisan Languages," *Encyclopaedia Britannica*, 22 (London: 1987) and later edns., and a somewhat longer introduction in Tom Güldemann and Rainer Vossen, "Khoisan," in *African Languages: An Introduction*, ed. Bernd Heine and Derek Nurse (Cambridge: Cambridge University Press, 2000). Contributions referred to in the text are Dorothea F. Bleek, "A Short Survey of Bushman Languages," *Zeitschrift für Eingeborenen-Sprachen*, 30 (1939–40): 52–72; Jürgen Christoph Winter, "Khoisan," in *Die Sprachen Afrikas*, ed. Bernd Heine *et al.*, (Hamburg: Helmut Buske Verlag, 1981), 329–74 (with a list of language names); Anthony Traill, *The Complete Guide to the Koon: A Research Report on Linguistic Fieldwork Undertaken in Botswana and South West Africa. Communications from the African Studies Institute, No 1*, (Johannesburg: University of the Witwatersrand, 1974).

Information about Australian languages is from R. M. W. Dixon, *The Languages of Australia* (Cambridge: Cambridge University Press, 1980).

On the areas needed to support gatherers and hunters v. farmers, see Colin Renfrew, *Archaeology and Language* (London: Cape, 1987). As for the number of languages in prehistoric times, see R. M. W. Dixon, *The Rise and Fall of Languages* (Cambridge: Cambridge University Press, 1997) and David Nettle, *Linguistic Diversity* (Oxford: Oxford University Press, 1999), ch. 5. Estimations of population size are provided and discussed in depth by Fekri A. Hassan, *Demographic Archaeology* (New York: Academic Press, 1981).

2. THE LARGE LANGUAGE GROUPS

Problems of how languages are related historically belong to the well-established discipline of historical linguistics. A very readable general introduction is Jean Aitchison, *Language Change: Progress or Decay?*, 2nd edn. (Cambridge: Cambridge University Press, 1991). More comprehensive works are R. L. Trask, *Historical Linguistics* (London: Arnold, 1996) and Winfred P. Lehmann, *Historical Linguistics*, 3rd edn. (London: Routledge, 1992); the latter covers the Indo-European group in detail.

The origin and spread of herding and farming is discussed in depth by Jared Diamond, *Guns, Germs and Steel* (London: Jonathan Cape, 1997).

Colin Renfrew, *Archaeology and Language* (London: Cape, 1987), and J. P. Mallory, *In Search of the Indo-Europeans: Language, Archaeology and Myth* (London: Thames & Hudson, 1989), represent two divergent views on how the Indo-European languages spread. Surveys of the language groups of the world are found in *The Cambridge Encyclopedia of Language* as well as in *International Encyclopedia of Linguistics*, both referred to above.

Further information and references on Bantu languages can be found in the article "Bantu Languages" by Benji Wald in *International Encyclopedia of Linguistics*. The standard grammar for Setswana (Tswana) is Desmond T. Cole, *An Introduction to Tswana Grammar* (Cape Town: Longmans, 1955) or later reprints.

A very interesting study of how languages in the same geographic area tend to share grammatical features is Joanna Nichols, *Linguistic Diversity in Space and Time* (Chicago: Chicago University Press, 1992).

3. WRITING AND THE EGYPTIANS

For the historical background to this and the two following chapters, an accessible overview is provided in Charles Freeman, *Egypt, Greece and Rome: Civilizations of the Ancient Mediterranean* (Oxford: Oxford University Press, 1996).

Further Reading

Early writing systems are surveyed in two recent works: Florian Coulmas, *The Blackwell Encyclopedia of Writing Systems* (Cambridge, Mass.: Blackwell, 1996) and Peter T. Daniels and William Bright, *The World's Writing Systems* (Oxford: Oxford University Press, 1995).

A first introduction to hieroglyphs is W. V. Davies, *Egyptian Hieroglyphs* (London: British Museum, 1987), which is the source for the examples in the text. A more substantial handbook is Mark Collier and Bill Manley, *How to Read Egyptian Hieroglyphs: A Step-by-Step Guide to Teach Yourself* (London: British Museum Press, 1998).

4. GREEK AND THE GREEKS

The texts written by the ancient Greek and Latin authors mentioned in this and the following chapter are all published in Loeb Classical Library (original texts and facing English translation).

A full treatment of the history of the Greek language from its beginnings to the present time is found in Geoffrey Horrocks, *Greek: A History of the Language and Its Speakers* (London and New York: Longman, 1997).

How the influence from Egypt and the East on early Greek culture was denied by Western scholars is treated in detail by Martin Bernal, *Black Athena: The Afroasiatic Roots of Classical Civilization*, i. *The Fabrication of Ancient Greece 1785–1985* (New Brunswick: Rutgers University Press, 1987). Bernal also advances highly controversial ideas about the actual extent of that influence.

5. LATIN AND THE ROMANS

A history of ancient Latin is found in Leonard R. Palmer, *The Latin Language* (London: Faber & Faber, 1954). E. Polomé, "The Linguistic Situation in the Western Provinces of the Roman Empire," in *Aufstieg und Niedergang der römischen Welt*, ed. H. Temporini and W. Haase, (Berlin: de Gruyter, 1983), II. 29. 2, 509–53, treats other languages in the

Roman Empire. For medieval Latin there is now a large modern overview in English, F. A. C. Mantello and A. G. Rigg, *Medieval Latin: An Introduction and Bibliographical Guide* (Washington, DC: The Catholic University of America Press, 1996).

6. DID DANTE WRITE IN ITALIAN?

For the historical background to this and the following chapter, see e.g. *The Oxford Illustrated History of Medieval Europe*, ed. George Holmes (Oxford: Oxford University Press, 1988). On the transition from Latin to French, see Roger Wright, *Late Latin and Early Romance in Spain and Carolingian France* (Liverpool: Cairns, 1982). The relations between Latin and the new languages and language names are discussed in Tore Janson, "Language Change and Metalinguistic Change: Latin to Romance and Other Cases," in *Latin and the Romance Languages in the Early Middle Ages*, ed. Roger Wright (London: Routledge, 1991, repr. 1996), 19–28. Dante's treatise on language is available in a new English translation: Steven Botterill, *Dante Alighieri: De Vulgari Eloquentia* (Cambridge: Cambridge University Press, 1996). The English version of the first lines of *La divina commedia* is taken from the translation by Charles S. Singleton.

7. FROM GERMANIC TO MODERN ENGLISH

The early German groups and their languages are the subject of Orrin W. Robinson, *Old English and Its Closest Relatives: A Survey of the Earliest Germanic Languages* (Stanford: Stanford University Press, 1992). The standard work on the runes of England is R. I. Page, *An Introduction to English Runes* (London: Methuen, 1973).

The law of Ethelbert is accorded little attention in most works on the English language. The extract is quoted from the edition by F. Liebermann, *Die Gesetze Der Angelsachsen* (3 vols.; Halle: Niemeyer, 1903–16).

Further Reading

An excellent introduction to early English language and literature is Bruce Mitchell and Fred C. Robinson, *A Guide to Old English*, 5th edn. (Oxford: Blackwell, 1992). The poem *Beowulf* has been discussed in innumerable publications and rendered into modern English many times, most recently by Seamus Heaney (London: Faber, 2000). The *Ecclesiastical History* by Bede is most easily accessible in the edition in the Loeb Classical Library.

There are several good surveys of the history of the English language. Albert C. Baugh and Thomas Cable, *A History of the English Language*, 3rd edn. (London: Routledge & Kegan Paul, 1978) gives much attention to social and historical facts, but is not wholly up to date. Dennis Freeborn, *From Old English to Standard English*, 2nd edn. (London: Macmillan, 1998) is a textbook with much discussion of language variation. *The Cambridge History of the English Language*, ed. Richard M. Hogg (Cambridge: Cambridge University Press 1992–9), is a monumental summary of the present state of knowledge, in 5 vols.

8. THE ERA OF NATIONAL LANGUAGES

The decision of the Brewer's Guild is quoted from Christopher Allmand, *Henry V* (Berkeley and Los Angeles: University of California Press, 1992), 424. There is an excellent discussion of the use of Latin in the post-medieval period in Peter Burke, *The Art of Conversation* (Cambridge: Polity Press, 1993), ch. 2.

The development of national languages is treated most fully in histories of the respective languages; for English, see above. The creation of nation states and the nature of nationalism are topics that have been discussed intensely in the last decades by historians, anthropologists, and others. A few important works are Anthony D. Smith, *The Ethnic Origin of Nations* (Oxford: Blackwell, 1986), Benedict Anderson, *Imagined Communities: Reflections on the Origin and Spread of Nationalism*, revised edn. (London and New York: Verso, 1991), and

Charles Tilly, *Coercion, Capital, and European States,* AD 990–1992 (Cambridge, Mass. and Oxford: Blackwell, 1992).

9. LANGUAGES OF EUROPE AND OF THE WORLD

A survey of the European expansion of trade is found in Eric R. Wolf, *Europe and the People without History* (Berkeley, Los Angeles, London: University of California Press, 1997), Part 2 (chs. 5–8). The ecological effects, including the decimation or extinction of populations, are discussed in Alfred W. Crosby, *Ecological Imperialism: The Biological Expansion of Europe, 900–1900* (Cambridge: Cambridge University Press, 1986).

10. HOW LANGUAGES ARE BORN—OR MADE

There are several introductions to the field of Creole and pidgin languages, e.g. John Holm, *Pidgins and Creoles* (2 vols.; Cambridge: Cambridge University Press, 1988–9), from which the example of Nevis Creole is taken. For Afrikaans most literature is in Afrikaans or German, except the controversial book by Marius F. Valkhoff, *Studies in Portuguese and Creole, with Special Reference to South Africa* (Johannesburg: University of the Witwatersrand, 1966), describing Afrikaans as a Creole language. For Norwegian, see Einar Haugen, *The Scandinavian Languages* (London: Faber, 1976). For the history of the Sotho languages, see Tore Janson and Joseph Tsonope, *Birth of a National Language: The History of Setswana* (Gaborone: Heinemann, 1991), ch. 4.

11. HOW LANGUAGES DISAPPEAR

There are some good recent books on language extinction: David Crystal, *Language Death* (Cambridge: Cambridge University Press, 2000) and Suzanne Romaine and Daniel Nettle, *Vanishing Voices: The*

Further Reading

Extinction of the World's Languages (Oxford: Oxford University Press, 2000). The fate of East Sutherland Gaelic is described in Nancy Dorian, *Language Death: The Life Cycle of a Scottish Gaelic Dialect* (Philadelphia: University of Pennsylvania Press, 1981). The quote from Patrick Sellar is found in *Papers on Sutherland Estate Management, 1802–1816*, ed. R. J. Adams (Edinburgh: 1972), i. 175. The languages of New Guinea are treated in William A. Foley, *The Papuan Languages of New Guinea* (Cambridge: Cambridge University Press, 1986). On Shiyeyi and Thimbukushu, see Lars-Gunnar Andersson and Tore Janson, *Languages in Botswana: Language Ecology in Southern Africa* (Gaborone: Longman Botswana, 1997).

12. THE HEYDAY OF ENGLISH

The histories of English mentioned above discuss the expansion of the language. An overview of the rise of English is provided by David Crystal, *English as a Global Language* (Cambridge: Cambridge University Press, 1997). Robert Phillipson, *Linguistic Imperialism* (Oxford: Oxford University Press, 1992) and *Post-Imperial English*, ed. Joshua Fishman et al. (New York etc.: Mouton de Gruyter, 1996) treat the present worldwide dominance from different perspectives. The figures for speakers of large languages are taken from *Ethnologue*; see beginning of this section.

13. AND THEN?

The future of languages has not been the subject of much previous speculation. However, the imminent danger facing many languages of the world is discussed in the books on language extinction mentioned above. The works about English listed in the previous section all have something about the future of English. See also Daniel Nettle, *Linguistic Diversity* (Oxford: Oxford University Press, 1999).

Index

Aasen, Ivar 222
Aborigines, *see* Australian languages
Académie française 178
Adam 1–2, 119
Aeneid, the 89
Aeolic dialect 78–80
Aeschylus 80
Africa 40, 44–5, 51, 54, 187, 197, 200–1
    number of languages 240, 243
    see also West Africa; northern Africa; southern Africa
Afrikaans 20, 214–20, 265
Afro-Asiatic languages 51, 55
Agricola 133
agriculture 39–46, 57–9, 186, 188
Akkadian 50, 59
Albania 90
Albanian 36
Alexander the Great 60, 81
Alfred the Great 149, 162
Algeria 95
Almohads, the 166
alphabetic script 70–2
America 49, 186, 189–90, 193–6, 200–1
    number of languages 240, 242

    see also Central America; North America; South America
American Indian languages 13, 26–7, 52, 75, 186, 190–1, 242
anatomy of vocal organs 3–5
Angles 130–4, 148
Angola 197
Arabic 42, 96, 111, 167, 201
Aragón 167
Aramaic 82
archaeology 3–5
Argentina 189, 190
Aristotle 72–3
Armenian 83
Asia 39, 42, 51–2, 188, 197–8, 200–1
    number of languages 240, 243
Asturias 167
Athens 78, 80
Attic dialect 78–80
Attila 42
Augustine, Archbishop of Canterbury 139–40, 142
Augustus, Roman emperor 92
Australia 199
    number of languages 26, 199, 242

Index

Australian languages 14–15, 26,
    75, 199, 242
Austronesian languages 51, 53
Aymara 190

Babel 75, 119
Babylon 59
Baltic languages 36
Bantu languages 44–8, 55
Basque 49, 94, 189
Bede, the Venerable 146–8
Belarus 33
Bengali 201
Beowulf 143–4
Bertha, Queen of Kent 139, 141,
    142
Bible, the 1–2, 82, 119
Bible translation:
    Afrikaans 216
    Danish 169, 220
    disappearing languages 238
    English 169
    Sepedi 227
    Sesotho 227
    Setswana 226
    Swedish 169, 175
birth of languages 124–6, 202–31
    see also names of languages
Bleek, Dorothea 19
Boas, Franz 75
Boccaccio, Giovanni 173
Boers 215–17, 228
Boileau, Nicolas 177

Bolivia 189, 190
Bologna, language/dialect of 121
Borneo 51, 53
Botswana 47, 224–9, 245–7
Brazil 184–7
Breton 94
Brewers' Guild, the 165
Breytenbach, Breyten 217
Brink, André 217
Britain 96, 129–64, 256–7, 264–6
British (Brythonic) 129, 131, 136
British Council, the 264
Brythonic, see British
Bulgarian 33
Bushmen, see San people
Byzantine Empire, the 83–4

Cabral, Pedro 184–5, 196
Caedmon 147
Caesar, Gaius Iulius 91–2
Calderón, Pedro 174
Cambodia 198
Cambridge University 264
Cameroon 44
Canada 191
Cape of Good Hope 185, 214
Casalis, Eugène 226
Castile 167
Castilian 167
    see also Spanish
Catalan 167, 189
Catholic Church, see Church
Caxton, Willliam 160

Celtic languages 35–6, 94,
    129–31, 232–5
Central African Republic 265
Central America 39, 52, 188–9,
    242
Cervantes, Miguel de 174
change (of languages) 30–2, 38,
    53–5, 213–14, 276
  rate 156
Charlemagne 111
Charles the Bald 112–13
Chaucer, Geoffrey 160, 174
Chile 189
China 39–40
Chinese 51–2, 56, 201
  Cantonese 198
  Mandarin 260
  writing system 66–8, 281
Christianity 95, 260
  see also Bible, the; Church
Church:
  Catholic vs. Protestant 102,
    169–71
  Christian 138, 139–42, 144,
    150–1, 168
  English 233
Cicero, Marcus Tullius 91–3, 173
click sounds 14, 19
Colombia 189
colonial languages 82, 187, 197
Columbus, Christopher 184–5
communications 115, 189, 192,
    237, 239, 241, 258, 276–7

competition between languages
    179–83
complexity of languages 14–15
Constantine the Great 83
Coptic 83
Corneille, Pierre 174–5
Cornish 129
Creole languages 206–14, 219,
    269
cuneiform script 59, 66, 72
Curaçao 209
Cyrillic alphabet 33
Czech 33
Czech republic, the 272

Danish 31, 169, 220
Danish-Norwegian 221–2
Dante Alighieri 118–28, 173
Darwinism 8
daughter language 50
death of languages 234
  see also disappearance of
    languages
definition of "language" 23–4,
    108–11, 207–10
definition of "language family"
    49–50
definition of "language group"
    50
Descartes, René 102
determinatives 64–5
development of languages
    12–18, 74–8

dialects 26, 78–80, 86–7, 101,
    145, 196, 217, 236–7
    see also divergence
Diaz, Bartholomeu 185
dimotiki 84–5, 87, 223
disappearance of languages
    96–8, 199, 232–50
diseases 189
divergence of dialects/languages
    31, 60–1, 163–4, 273, 280
Dixon, R. M. W. 15
Dorian, Nancy 234
Doric dialect 80, 87
Dravidian languages 52
Dutch 215, 219
    in North America 190
    in Surinam 195
Dylan, Bob 258

East Sutherland 232–4
Easter Island 51
Ecuador 189
education, *see* schools
Egypt 57–68, 72, 81, 90
Egyptian 3, 57–68
England, *see* Britain
English 13, 24, 29–32, 38, 129–64,
    169, 171, 255–66, 271–4
    in Asia 198
    in Australia and New Zealand
    198–9
    change of 156–7
    in North America 190–3

Old English 31–2, 36, 38,
    129–51
    see also international
    languages
Eritrea 50
Estonian 51
Ethelbert, King of Kent 139–42,
    147, 162
Ethiopia 39, 50
Etruscan 93
Etruscan alphabet 91, 161
Euripides 80
Europe *passim; see especially*
    32–44, 99–107, 166–83,
    184–201
    number of languages 96–7,
    163, 240, 243
European languages 13, 32,
    74–5, 105–7, 164–83,
    184–201
    see also Indo-European
    languages
European Union, the 104–5
Eve 119
evolution of man 7–8
extinction of languages, *see*
    disappearance of languages

Farsi 36
Fertile Crescent, the 42, 50
film 258
finance 259
Finnish 51, 152–3

France 49, 93, 108–28
Frederick II 118
French 34, 108–28, 170, 172, 173
   advanced 212
   in North America 191
   Old French 114
   see also international
     languages
Frisian 162
functionality of languages 77
future of languages 267–82

Gaelic 130, 232–4
Galicia 167
Gama, Vasco da 184
gatherers and hunters 10–28
Genghis Khan 42
German 29–32, 119, 170, 172,
   265
   Old High German 31–2
   see also international
     languages
Germanic, *see* Proto-Germanic
Germanic languages 31–2, 35–6,
   38, 56
   change 157
Germany 266
Goa 198
God 1–2
Gothic 99
Gotland, language/dialect of
   162–3
graffiti 93

Greece 69–88, 90
Greek 35–8, 60, 69–88, 167–8,
   172
   alphabet 70–1, 161, 281
   Byzantine 85
   Modern 85
Gregory the Great, Pope 139–40
Guinea-Bissau 197

Haiti 195
Haitian 195, 209
Hausa 244
Hawaii 51
Hebrew 75, 238–9
Hellenes 79
Henry V, King of England 160,
   165
Henry VIII, King of England
   169
hieroglyphs 62–8, 72
Hindi 36, 201, 260
historical linguistics 53–5
   see also change
Hittite 36
Homo sapiens sapiens 4
Horace (Quintus Horatius
   Flaccus) 91–2
Hundred Years War, the 153
Hungarian 51, 119
Hungary 51, 272
Huns, the 42
hunters, *see* gatherers and
   hunters

Iberian Peninsula 166–7
Iberoromance 167
Ibsen, Henrik 221
Iceland 266
Icelandic 31, 279
identity through language 23,
    76, 128, 155, 192, 214, 280
Igbo 244
Iliad, the 72
Inca Empire 188
India 40, 52, 82, 198
Indian languages, *see* American
    Indian languages
Indochina 198
Indo-European languages
    35–44, 55
Indonesia 51, 198
Ine, King of Wessex 143
international languages 251–66
    English 256–66, 270–3
    French 177–9, 254
    German 254–5
    Latin 99–105, 168–73, 177–9
    Russian 255–6
Inuit 191
Iran 81
Iranian languages 36
Iraq 42
Ireland 90
Irian Jaya 241
Irish 35, 130
    Old Irish 36
Isixhosa, *see* Xhosa

Isizulu, *see* Zulu
Islam 96, 260
Israel 42
Italian 29, 34, 108–28, 170, 173
Italic languages 36

Japanese 49, 56, 201
    writing system 68
Jesus 82
John, King of England 153
Jones, Sir William 35
Ju|'hoan 15–18
Jutes 135

Kannada 52
kathareuousa 84–5, 87, 223
Kenya 244, 266
Khoekhoegowab 11
Khoisan languages 11–28, 269
Kiswahili, *see* Swahili
knights' schools 172
Knudsen, Knud 221
koine 81

Lagerlöf, Selma 175
Laos 198
large languages, term 25
Latin 34, 35–8, 82, 89–107,
    108–28, 130–1, 167, 168, 172
    alphabet 47, 91, 139, 161, 281
    see also international
        languages
Leibniz, G. W. von 102

Lennon, John 258
León 167
Lesbos 69, 78
Lesotho 224–9
Libya 95
Linear B 72
linguistic imperialism 264
literature 17, 75, 143–6, 173–6
loanwords 77, 158, 181, 262
logographic writing systems
    66–8
Lothar 112
Louis the German 112–14
Louis XIV, King of France 177
Louis the Pious 112
Luther, Martin 169

Ma'anyan languages 53
Macao 198
Macedonia 81
Macedonian 81
Madagascar 51, 53
Magalhâes, Fernâo de 187
Magellan, *see* Magalhâes
Malagasy 53
Malayalam 52
Maori 200
Marshall Plan, the 257
mass media 237
Maya culture and script 188
Mexico 39, 189, 266
minority languages 249, 252–3
Moffat, Robert 226

Molière (Jean Baptiste Poquelin)
    174
Mongols, the 42
Montaigne, Michel de 173
Mozambique 197, 265
music, vocal 258
Mussolini, Benito 89

Nama 11
names of languages 20–23,
    124–6, 225–8, 230
Namibia 11, 265
Napoleon Bonaparte 89
nation states 161–4
national languages 161–4,
    165–83
Navarra 167
Neanderthal man 5
Near East (Western Asia) 39–43,
    50, 72
negation, double 218
Nero, Roman emperor 92
Nevis 206
New Granada 189
New Guinea 39, 240–2
New Spain 189
New Zealand 51, 200
Newton, Isaac 102
Nigeria 244, 266
Nijmegen, peace treaty of 178
Nithard 112, 114
Nordic (Scandinavian) languages
    31, 220

Index

Norman French 151–5
Norse, Old 31–2, 36, 38
North America 40, 52, 190–1, 203,
Northern Sotho, *see* Sepedi
northern Africa 42, 90, 167, 201
Norwegian 24, 31, 109, 220–4
Nostratic 55
number of languages 25–8, 195, 200–1, 235–6
  on continents 240–5
  in Europe 163

Occitan 116, 120, 162
Odyssey, the 72
ogham 161
Oliva, peace treaty of 178
Orange Free State 215
origin of languages 1–10
Oscan 93
Ottoman Empire, the 84
Oxford University 264

Pacific, the 240
Palestine 90
Papiamentu 209
Papua New Guinea 241
parent language 50
Pedi, *see* Sepedi
Perrault, Charles 177
Persian 36
person, in grammar 13
Peru 189, 190

Petrarch (Francesco Petrarca) 173
Pictish 131, 136
Picts 130
pidgin languages 205–7
Pizarro, Fransisco 188
Plato 72–3, 78
poetry 69–71
Polish 33
popular languages 182
Portugal 93, 122, 167
Portuguese 34, 49, 167, 186–7, 265
  in Africa 196–7
  in Asia 197–8
  Brazilian 187
prefixes 47
primitive languages 75
Protestant Churches, *see* Church
Proto-Germanic 31–2, 38, 134
Proto-Indo-European 39, 107
  see also Indo-European languages
proto-languages 50, 55
Proto-Nordic 31
Proto-Slavic 33, 38
Provençal 116, 118, 120
Puritans, the 171
pyramids 60–1

Quebec 191
Quechua 190, 195
querelle des anciens et des modernes 177

Rabelais, François 173
Racine, Jean 174–5, 177
Rastadt, peace treaty of 178
rebus principle 64
reconstruction of languages
    54–5
religions and languages 260
Rembarrnga 14
Renaissance, the 176
Renfrew, Colin 43
rhetoric 92
Riebeeck, Jan van 215, 217
Rio de la Plata 189
Roman Empire, the 82–3
Romance languages 34, 36,
    108–28
Romania 94, 122
Romans, the 89–107
Rome 89–107
runes, runic script 136–8, 139,
    142
    Anglo-Saxon 137–8
    Germanic 161
Russian 32–3
    see also international
        languages

Saami languages 243
Sallust (Gaius Sallustius Crispus)
    92
San people 10–28, 75
Sanskrit 35–8
Sappho 69, 72, 78

Sardic 121
Sardinia 94, 121
Saxons 130, 134, 148
Scandinavian languages, *see*
    Nordic languages
schools and education 95, 100–1,
    228–9, 237, 239, 252, 263,
    276
    and national languages
        167–73
science 72, 102, 159, 182, 259
Scotland 90
Scots (English) 164
Scots Gaelic 130, 131, 136
Scottish, *see* Scots Gaelic
Second Vatican Council 170
Sellar, Patrick 232
Semitic languages 50
Semitic scripts 70
Seneca, Lucius Annaeus 92
Sepedi 227–9
Serbo-Croatian 33
Sesotho 225–9
Setswana 47–8, 226–9, 245–7
Shakespeare, William 174–5
shift (to another language) 96–8,
    191–2
    see also disappearance of
        languages
Shiyeyi 245–7
Shona 244
Shuakhwe 20, 22
Siberia 51, 243

Sicilian 118, 121
Sicily 94
Sierra Leone 277
Sino-Tibetan languages 51
size of languages 25–8, 200–1,
    274
slaves, slave trade 192, 202–5
Slavic languages 32–3, 35, 36,
    119
Slavonic, Old Church 33
small languages, term 25
Socrates 73
Somalia 277
Sophocles 80
Sorbian 243
Sotho languages 224–9
    see also Sesotho
South Africa 20, 47, 216, 224–9,
    244
southern Africa 10, 44, 214, 224
South America 40, 52, 184–90,
    193–6
Soviet Union, the 255–6
Spain 49, 93, 167
Spanish (Castilian) 13, 34, 49,
    108–28, 167, 170
    in America 186–90
    in the United States 192
spread of languages 53–6, 81–2,
    93–4, 184–201, 274
stock-raising 39–46
Strasbourg, oaths of 112
Strindberg, August 175

Sumatra 51
Sumerian 3, 59
Surinam 195
Sutherland, Lady 232
Swahili 46, 48, 244
Swedish 24, 29–32, 109, 152–3
    in North America 190
Switzerland 94
sword, invention of 41
syllabic writing systems 68
Syria 42, 90
Syrian 83

Tacitus, Cornelius 92, 133–4
Tamil 52, 56
Tanzania 244
taxes 62, 94, 99, 171, 239
Telugu 52
Thimbukushu 245–7
Tok Pisin 241–2
Tordesillas, Treaty of 185
Traill, Anthony 21
Transvaal 215
Tsakonian 86–7
Tswana, *see* Setswana
Tunisia 95
Turkey 36, 42, 50, 81, 90
Tuscan 121

Ukrainian 33
Umbrian 93
United Kingdom, *see* Britain
United States 189, 257–9, 265–6

universities 168
Uralic languages 51, 55

value of languages 76
Vatican State, the 105
Vega, Lope de 174
Venezuela 189
Vera Cruz 184
verb forms 13, 207, 210–11,
    217–18
Vietnam 198
Vikings 149
Virgil (Publius Vergilius Maro)
    89, 91–2, 106, 173, 177
vocabulary 15–18, 73–7, 105–7,
    157–9, 181
vowels 13

Wales 94
Welsh 94, 129, 269

West Africa 39, 204
West African languages 212–13
West Indies 185
Western Asia, *see* Near East
written language and language
    name 124–6
Wycliffe, John 169

Xhosa 46, 48
!Xóõ 14, 23

Yemen 50
Yoruba 244

Zimbabwe 244
Zulu 46, 48
Zwingli, Huldrych 169